"A crown jewel in Paul's earthly ministry was the collection from gentile believers for impoverished Jewish Christians in Jesus' homeland. Murray J. Harris brings his world-class expertise in Paul, Acts, and 2 Corinthians to bear in telling this story. A full one-third of the book details the relevance of that long-ago collection for current outlook and practice. The result is an inspiring and exegetically rigorous commendation of responsive generosity toward others based on God's goodness and gifts to us."

—ROBERT W. YARBROUGH, professor of New Testament, Covenant Theological Seminary, St. Louis, Missouri

"With characteristic succinct clarity Murray Harris shines a light on Paul's long-planned collection of a gift for poor believers. Harris integrates the details of Acts with Paul's letters, guides readers through Paul's longest discussion of the collection (2 Cor 8—9), and offers wise practical insight into the complexities and blessings of giving and generosity. This book on a topic that is sometimes avoided or exploited is yet another gift to the church from Murray Harris."

—ALAN J. THOMPSON, head of New Testament, Sydney Missionary and Bible College, Sydney, Australia

"Paul's collection for the Jewish Christians in Jerusalem was a fundamental part of his ministry, but it is often overlooked when we think about Paul's mission work. Drawing on a lifetime of study of the New Testament, Murray Harris comes to our aid and shows us how very much we can learn from this overlooked feature of Paul's life. This engaging book about Paul's collection will enable us all to understand ministry, stewardship and practical giving in new ways and from fresh angles."

—PAUL TREBILCO, professor of New Testament studies, University of Otago, Dunedin, New Zealand

"For believers seeking to base their understanding of Christian stewardship on faithful and rigorous exegesis, I know of no better resource than Murray Harris's *Christian Stewardship in Light of Paul's Collection for the Poor*. Harris takes the reader on a 'deep dive' of an often-neglected subject."

—ROBERT L. PLUMMER, Collin and Evelyn Aikman Professor of Biblical Studies, The Southern Baptist Theological Seminary

Christian Stewardship in Light of Paul's Collection for the Poor

Christian Stewardship in Light of Paul's Collection for the Poor

MURRAY J. HARRIS

WIPF & STOCK · Eugene, Oregon

CHRISTIAN STWARDSHIP IN LIGHT OF PAUL'S COLLECTION FOR
THE POOR

Wipf & Stock
An Imprint of Wipf and Stock Publishers
199 W. 8th Ave., Suite 3
Eugene, OR 97401

www.wipfandstock.com

PAPERBACK ISBN: 979-8-3852-3503-2
HARDCOVER ISBN: 979-8-3852-3504-9
EBOOK ISBN: 979-8-3852-3505-6

12/11/24

To Peter B. Southwick,
a shining example of Christian stewardship

Contents

Preface

Life has been picturesquely described as a pilgrimage between two moments of nakedness—birth and death. "We brought nothing into the world, and we can take nothing out of it" (1 Tim 6:7). During the interval of uncertain length between those two fixed points, Christians have the opportunity and challenge of using their talents, time, and possessions for the benefit of others and the praise of God.

In the present volume, we shall be examining the apostle Paul's stewardship in using his gift of leadership and his concern for others—particularly from AD 52–57—in organizing financial relief aid for the poor within the church of Jerusalem. Hopefully this will serve as a model of stewardship for twenty-first-century Christians to emulate in our vastly different circumstances.

Acknowledgments

With the kind permission of the publishers, I have made use of material, usually with changes, found in my commentaries on 2 Corinthians: in *The Expositor's Bible Commentary: Romans to Galatians* (Grand Rapids: Zondervan, 1976 and 2008) and *The Second Epistle to the Corinthians: A Commentary on the Greek Text*, The New Testament International Greek Testament Commentary (Grand Rapids: Eerdmans, 2005). Also, permission was granted for use, with changes, of my article "Christian Stewardship," *Interest*, February 1979, 4–5.

All translations of ancient documents are my own, including Scriptural citations unless otherwise noted.

Yet again, I am indebted to my sterling friends of eighty years, David Burt and Dr. Graham D. Smith, for their perceptive and beneficial comments on this manuscript. Views expressed in the work and any errors that remain are my own.

It is a special pleasure for me to dedicate the present book to Peter B. Southwick, a friend who continues to show exemplary creativity in his community aid, especially toward the housing of Pacific Islanders who live in New Zealand.

Also, I gratefully acknowledge the skillful and patient editorial work at Wipf and Stock of Riley Bounds, Dr. Savanah N. Landerholm, Karlie Tedrick and Kyle Lundburg in preparing this book for publication.

Abbreviations

AD	*Anno Domini* (Latin), in the year of our Lord (= the Christian era)
BC	Before Christ
BDAG	*A Greek-English Lexicon of the New Testament and Other Early Christian Literature* (rev. and ed. F. W. Danker; Chicago/London: University of Chicago, 2000), based on W. Bauer's *Griechisch-deutsches Wörterbuch* (6th ed.) and on previous English eds. by W. F. Arndt, F. W. Gingrich, and F. W. Danker
	References are given by page number and by a–d (= the four sections of the page)
Bruce, *Acts*	F. F. Bruce, *The Book of Acts* (Grand Rapids: Eerdmans, 1988)
c.	*circa* (Latin) about
cf.	*confer* (Latin), compare
d.	died
EVV	English versions of the New Testament
GNT	Good News Translation (1992)
Harris, *2 Cor*	M. J. Harris, *The Second Epistle to the Corinthians: A Commentary on the Greek Text,* ed. I. H. Marshall and D. A. Hagner (Grand

	Rapids: Eerdmans/Milton Keyes: Paternoster, 2005)
Harris, *Corinth*	M. J. Harris, *Renowned—But . . . : The Church of Corinth in the First Century AD and Its Relevance for the Twenty-First-Century Church* (Eugene, OR: Wipf and Stock, 2022)
Harris, *Immortality*	M. J. Harris, *Raised Immortal: Resurrection and Immortality in the New Testament* (London: Marshall, Morgan & Scott, 1983/ Grand Rapids: Eerdmans, 1985)
Harris, *Prepositions*	M. J. Harris, *Prepositions and Theology in the Greek New Testament* (Grand Rapids: Zondervan, 2012)
Harris, *Questions*	M. J. Harris, *Three Crucial Questions About Jesus* (Grand Rapids: Baker, 1994/Eugene, Oregon: Wipf and Stock, 2008)
Harris, *Resurrection*	M. J. Harris, *From Grave to Glory: Resurrection in the New Testament* (Grand Rapids: Zondervan 1990)
Harris, *Slave*	M. J. Harris, *Slave of Christ: A New Testament Metaphor for Total Devotion to Christ* (Leicester: Apollos/Downers Grove, Illinois: InterVarsity, 1999)
Harris, *Texts (1)*	M. J. Harris, *Navigating Tough Texts: A Guide to Problem Passages in the New Testament; Volume 1* (Bellingham, Washington: Lexham, 2020)
Harris, *Texts (2)*	M. J. Harris, *Navigating Tough Texts: A Guide to Problem Passages in the New Testament; Volume 2* (Bellingham, Washington: Lexham, 2024)
LSB	Legacy Standard Bible (updated NASB) (2021)

LSJ	H. G. Liddell and R. Scott, *A Greek-English Lexicon* (9th ed.; rev. H. S. Jones et al.; Oxford: Clarendon,1940). *Supplement* (ed. E. A. Barber et al. Oxford: Clarendon, 1968)
LXX	Septuagint (= Greek Old Testament)
NASB	New American Standard Bible (1999)
NEB	New English Bible (1970)
NIDNTT	*The New International Dictionary of New Testament Theology,* 3 vols., ed. by Colin Brown (Grand Rapids: Zondervan/Exeter: Paternoster, 1975–78)
NIV	New International Version Bible (2011)
NJB	New Jerusalem Bible (1985)
NRSV	New Revised Standard Version Bible (1989)
NT	New Testament
OT	Old Testament
passim	(Latin) in many places
REB	Revised English Bible (1990)
TCNT	Twentieth Century New Testament (1904)

PART ONE

Paul's Collection for the Poor among Jerusalem Christians

During the years AD 52–57, the apostle Paul spent considerable time and effort in organizing a distinctive charity event,
his "collection for the poor among God's people in Jerusalem"
(Rom 15:26). He regarded this one-off offering by the largely gentile congregations in the churches he had begun as recognition of
their permanent indebtedness to their mother church in Jerusalem
from which the gospel had spread. Of the three passages in which
the apostle describes aspects of the collection (Rom 15:25–32; 1
Cor 16:1–4; 2 Cor 8–9), the two chapters in 2 Cor are founda-
tional and will form the basis of our whole discussion. In none
of his other letters does Paul devote such a prolonged treatment
(thirty-nine verses spread over two chapters!) to one topic—unambiguous evidence of the paramount importance he attached to
this collection.

I.

Chronology of the Collection

We can identify four primary stages in the formation of the collection.

A. STAGE 1 (ACTS 11) (AD 46)

On the basis of Paul's letters, it is impossible to know when the concept of a collection for destitute believers in Jerusalem may have entered Paul's thinking. But a passage in Acts—viz., 11:19–30—may suggest the genesis of the concept. The leaders of the Jerusalem church heard of the massive spread of the gospel in Syrian Antioch, including to Greeks, through the preaching of Jewish Christian evangelists from Cyprus and Cyrene. So they appointed Joseph, a Levite from Cyprus who had the nickname Barnabas (Acts 4:36), as their delegate to Antioch (Acts 11:20–22). Barnabas's probable assignment was to investigate how the Antiochene church was managing a mixed congregation of Jewish believers and uncircumcised gentiles. He discovered with pleasure the remarkable ongoing progress of the gospel there (Acts 11:23–24). On hearing of Saul's (= Paul's) gentile ministry in Cilician synagogues (cf. Gal 1:23–24), Barnabas went to Tarsus to invite Paul to join him at Antioch. During their joint ministry in the following year

(AD 45–46), Agabus, one of a group of prophets from Jerusalem, predicted that a severe famine would spread across the entire Roman world (Acts 11:25–28). Aware of the prophecy and no doubt already themselves feeling the effect of the famine, the Antiochene Christians organized a gift for their fellow believers in Judea, appointing (not surprisingly) Barnabas and Paul as their delegates (Acts 11:29–30; 12:25). On the reception of this gift in Jerusalem, see pp. 7–8 below.

How might this experience have triggered Paul's thought about a possible second relief visit to Jerusalem? He will have presumably seen:

- how believers could empathize with needy fellow believers elsewhere as an expression of Christian unity;

- how it was logistically possible to organize and transfer a gift (whether corn or money);

- the extent of the ongoing need in the Jerusalem church after personally hearing Agabus's prophecy about widespread famine;

- the mixed reaction among Jewish Christians in Jerusalem about receiving a gift from gentiles, albeit within a mixed Jewish–gentile congregation (note Paul's later unease expressed in Romans 15:31b); and

- the advisability of having more than one delegate with any gift and the importance of his personal involvement at every stage.

Most important of all, if the Acts 11 visit to Jerusalem is identical with the visit mentioned in Gal 2:1–3, 6–10 (as is probable), both occurring in AD 46, Paul will have remembered the request (not a directive) of the Jerusalem leadership triumvirate of James, Peter, and John, "that we should continue to remember the poor" (*tōn ptōchōn hina mnēmoneuōmen*) (Gal 2:10a). As Paul recollects that request, he immediately comments, "This is the very action I had already been eager to carry out" (Gal 2:10b), presumably referring to his Acts 11:30 visit to Jerusalem with Barnabas (Gal 2:1, 9). "Paul's Collection for the Poor" was his response to the Jerusalem leaders' request that he should continue his relief aid. (On the significance of Gal 2:10, see further below, pp. 13–15, 20–21).

B. STAGE 2 (ACTS 15) (AD 49)

The second important date is AD 49, when Paul makes his third post-conversion visit to Jerusalem. (The two previous post-conversion visits were in AD 35 [Acts 9:26–30; Gal 1:18–24] and AD 46. See pp. 3–4 above, and for a suggested chronology of Paul's life and letters, see Harris, *Paul*, 11–13.) For this third visit, Paul, Barnabas, and others were appointed to attend what is called the Jerusalem Council (Acts 15:2–29; Gal 2:4–5), where Jewish-gentile relations were discussed.

The Pharisaic party of believers had argued that gentile male believers must meet a twofold requirement to be eligible for salvation—be circumcised and adhere to Mosaic law (Acts 15:1, 5). Vigorous discussion on the issue focused in particular on Peter, Barnabas, Paul, and James (Acts 15:7–21), although the whole Jerusalem church was involved (Acts 15:12, 22). In a letter addressed to "the gentile believers in Antioch, Syria, and Cilicia" (Acts 15:23), the verdict of the Council was summed up: "It seemed appropriate to the Holy Spirit and to us not to burden you with any requirements beyond these essentials—that you abstain from food sacrificed to idols and from blood and from the meat of strangled animals and from sexual immorality. If you avoid these things, you will do well. Farewell" (Acts 15:28–29). The delivery of the letter was entrusted to Judas, Silas, Paul, and Barnabas. As Paul reflected on the outcome of the Council with its unambiguous endorsement of the gentile mission and affirmation that circumcision and adherence to Mosaic law were not necessary for salvation, he may well have realized that another relief gift for the poor among Jerusalem believers might further enhance harmonious relations with the mother church in Jerusalem and be a positive witness to unbelieving Jews in Jerusalem and elsewhere (cf. Rom 15:31a). In addition, his firsthand acquaintance with the ravaging effects in

Jerusalem of the widespread famine could well have intensified his commitment to possible relief measures.

C. STAGE 3 (ACTS 18) (AD 52)

The apostle's fourth post-conversion visit to Jerusalem in AD 52 is briefly mentioned in Acts 18:22: "When he had landed at Caesarea, he went up to Jerusalem, greeted the church there, and then went down to Antioch." The secondary Western text of Acts 18:21 suggests that Paul was keen to reach Jerusalem in time for one of the Jewish feasts. Whether or not that was the case, we may legitimately infer another purpose for Paul's brief visit to the mother church by considering Acts 18:23 that indicates that after spending some time in Antioch, Paul traveled "throughout the region of Galatia and Phrygia, strengthening all the disciples." It will have been at this time that Paul gave the Galatian churches certain instructions about the collection. To the Corinthians he says (in spring AD 55), "Follow the directions I gave to the churches of Galatia [in AD 52]" (1 Cor 16:1). These directions are set out in the next verse: "On the first day of every week, each one of you should set aside a sum of money in keeping with your income" (1 Cor 16:2).

If Paul already had a collection in mind at this time, it would have been natural for him to inform the Jerusalem leaders of his intention to initiate such a project in fulfillment of their own earlier wish expressed at the time of the "famine visit" (of Acts 11:29–30): "All they asked was that we should continue to remember the poor" (Gal 2:10).

At some stage during Paul's third missionary journey (AD 52–57; Acts 18:23–21:14), he must have informed the Macedonian churches such as Philippi, Thessalonica and Beroea (Acts 20:1–2) of the relief fund and requested their cooperation (cf. Acts 19:22). Rom 15:26 indicates that both Macedonia and Achaia (= Corinth, Cenchreae and others) "were pleased to make a contribution for the poor among God's people in Jerusalem."

D. STAGE 4 (ACTS 21) (AD 57)

Paul's fifth post-conversion visit to Jerusalem, his last visit, occurred probably in May AD 57 when he delivered the collection to the Jerusalem church.

Some scholars have argued that Acts does not explicitly refer to the collection because the Jerusalem leaders were unwilling to accept it until Paul had proved he was not against Mosaic law by paying the required expenses of the four poor Nazarites (Acts 21:21–24). But before the seven days of purification were over, some Asian Jews enticed the local populace to seize Paul, a seizure that led to prolonged custody (Acts 21:27—22:29), so the required offering was not paid at the temple and the collection was not accepted.

There is, however, no evidence that the Jerusalem leadership made their acceptance of the collection in any sense conditional. A strong case may be made for interpreting Acts 21:17–20 as an account of the warm receipt of the collection by the Jerusalem leadership. (On the issue of the purported silence of Acts, see further below, p. 17).

- With the phrase "to/at Jerusalem" (*eis Hierosolyma*) appearing in verses 15 and 17 of Acts 21, it is probable that verse 17 begins a new paragraph (vv. 17–26), so that the plural "brothers (and sisters)" (*hoi adelphoi*) is prospective, anticipating the reference to "James and all the elders" in verse 18 who then are included among "the brothers" who welcomed the delegation "with delight" (*asmenōs*). In that case, verse 17 describes an unofficial, informal welcome, while verse 18 describes the official and formal reception by the church; "all the elders were present" suggests formality.

- Paul's report of his ministry among the gentiles (v. 19) was detailed, "item by item" (*kath' hen hekaston*), which must have included a description of the collection that had just been delivered and even an indication of the stages of its formation. This report prompted all the hearers to praise

7

God. Interestingly, the same verb (*doxazō*, "praise") is used in Acts 21:20a ("they praised God") and in 2 Cor 9:13 ("others will praise God . . . for your generosity") regarding the recipients' response (past or future) to the collection.

- In his defense before Antonius Felix (Acts 24:1–27), Paul indirectly refers to the collection: "After several years, I came to Jerusalem to bring alms to my people and to present offerings" (Acts 24:17). Clearly, Luke was aware of Paul's relief aid so that it would have been natural for him to allude to it when Paul arrived in Jerusalem with the deputies of the churches. Why Luke avoids referring to the collection explicitly in Acts 21:17–20 is unclear. Perhaps he wanted to prevent his gentile readers (cf. Luke 1:3; Acts 1:1) from gaining wrong impressions about the nature or purpose of the collection—for example, they could have thought that it was a tax imposed by the mother church on its daughter churches or that it was some form of bribe on the Jerusalem church engineered by the gentile churches.

E. SUMMARY

Four of Paul's five visits to Jerusalem after his conversion (the first was in AD 35 and the last in AD 57) in some way involved his collection for the poor:

AD 46 Relief fund delivered from Antioch; Paul agrees to continue remembering the poor

AD 49 Collection plan seemingly crystallized in Paul's thinking

AD 52 Informing the Jerusalem leaders of his plan

AD 57 Delivering the relief fund

II.

Motivation for the Collection

What circumstances prompted Paul to spend a considerable portion of his time and energies over five years (AD 52–57) in organizing relief aid for impoverished fellow believers within the church of Jerusalem? And what inspired gentile Christians throughout the Roman Empire to help to alleviate the needs of destitute Messianic Jews living in the Holy City?

A. THE TEACHING OF JESUS

For Jesus, "the poor" may refer to the economically poor ("be generous to the poor," Luke 11:41), those who lack sufficient food, clothing, or housing for normal life. He realized that in this sense, "the poor you will always have with you" (Mark 14:7; cf. Deut 15:11; John 12:8). But "the poor" could also denote "the poor in spirit" (Matt 5:3), "those who are humble and contrite in spirit" (Isa 66:2), those who humbly recognize their spiritual poverty and their total dependence on God.

When Jesus instructs his disciples, "Sell your possessions and give to the poor" (Luke 12:33), he is addressing the general issue of anxiety over possessions (Luke 12:22–34). To achieve full dependence on God, people may need to dispose of encumbering possessions (he did not say "all" possessions) and give to the poor the result of the sale, thus gaining secure treasure in heaven (cf. Matt 19:21).

A distinctive feature of Jesus's view of stewardship is his total alignment with the poor and needy as recipients of care. To give to those in need is to give to Christ; to rob the poor of the help they need is to rob Christ himself.

- "Whatever you did for one of the least of these brothers and sisters of mine, you did for me" (Matt 25:40; cf. Prov 19:17, "Whoever is kind to the poor lends to the Lord and will be repaid in full").

- "Whatever you did not do for one of the least of these, you did not do for me" (Matt 25:45).

Similarly, to help God's people is to love God himself: "God is not so unjust as to forget your work and the love you have shown him when you have helped his people and continue to help them" (Heb 6:10).

B. THE TEACHING OF PAUL—SEE PART TWO

In what follows, pp. 10–19, I am using material, with changes, found in my commentary on *The Second Epistle to the Corinthians* (Grand Rapids: Eerdmans, 2005); used by permission.

C. WIDESPREAD FAMINE

In Acts 11:27–28, Luke indicates that "during this time" (AD 44–45) one of the prophets who had come down from Jerusalem to Antioch, named Agabus, through the Spirit predicted that a severe famine would spread over the entire Roman world. The expression (literally) "the inhabited world" (here *tēn oikoumenēn*) was a common Roman exaggeration for the Roman Empire as an administrative unit (cf. Luke 2:1; Acts 17:6; 24:5). Luke adds, "This happened during the reign of Claudius" (viz., AD 41–54). The reference is not simply to sporadic and regional food shortages but to a colossal empire-wide food crisis.

Independent testimony to this famine is found in several sources. For example:

- Pliny the Elder notes that with a massive rise in the height of the Nile's floodwaters in AD 45, the influence of a scant harvest was felt throughout Egypt and the Roman Empire; acute grain shortage led to inflated prices for grain.[1]

- Josephus records an episode during a drastic famine in Judea (around AD 46–48) when Queen Helena of Adiabene on her way to worship in Jerusalem observed many people dying of starvation and responded by sending some of her servants to Alexandria to buy grain at great expense and others to Cyprus to bring back a cargo of dried figs.[2]

- Both Tacitus[3] and Suetonius[4] refer to scarcity of grain during the reign of Claudius, resulting in famine.

This great famine, brought on by crop failures in North Africa, Egypt, Syria, and Judea, the breadbasket of the Roman Empire, lasted from AD 44 until about AD 63 when grain prices leveled out. During this time, the famine would have been aggravated by the sabbatical year, beginning in the fall AD 47 when land would lie fallow. But the financial relief needed by many within the Jerusalem church was intensified by certain unavoidable and unrelenting circumstances (see D immediately below).

D. ONGOING NEED IN JERUSALEM

- With the constant influx of Jewish converts (Acts 2:41, 47; 4:4; 6:7; 9:31; 21:1–4), many of them probably drawn

---

1. Pliny, *Naturalis Historia* 5.58.
2. Josephus, *Antiquities* 20.51–53.
3. Tacitus, *Annals* 12.43.
4. Suetonius, *Claudius* 18.2.

from the poorest classes of the city, the resources of the church were continually pressed, particularly because some of those converts were ostracized socially and economically as a result of their conversion (cf. Acts 8:1; 9:1–2). Also, from Acts 6:1–4, we learn that at the time when seven deacons were appointed "to serve tables" (= to care for the physical needs of the poor), the Hellenistic Jews "complained against the Hebraic Jews because their [= the Hellenistic] widows were being overlooked in the daily distribution of food" (Acts 6:1).

- Luke twice refers to a voluntary sharing of proceeds from the sale of goods and property (Acts 2:44–45; 4:34–35). This was not a reckless liquidation of capital assets but an economic necessity to guarantee corporate survival. No fewer than six "iterative imperfects" occur in Acts 2:45 and 4:34–35 that indicate that the believers *were in the habit of* supplementing the common fund from time to time as needs arose. Personal possessions were not regarded as private property to be used only for oneself (Acts 4:32). This display of voluntary generosity was unlike the required surrender of personal possessions on admission to the community of Essenes at Qumran.[5] Such communal sharing did intensify the poverty that had become a feature of the Jerusalem church.

- Simply living in Jerusalem in the first century AD brought financial challenges. At the city gates, customs duties were levied on agricultural items for sale within the city. Fruit purchased in Jerusalem cost three to six times its price in the country—and during a famine, the already inflated normal prices could multiply up to sixteen times.

- Palestinian Jews faced a crippling twofold taxation which in the first century AD may have been between 30 and 40 percent of total income—a tribute tax (*phoros*, Luke 20:22) or capitation tax (*kēnsos*, Matt 22:17) that was paid

---

5. Josephus, *Jewish War* 2.122.

to the emperor in Roman coin, and the annual temple tax (*didrachmon*, Matt 17:24) that was levied on every male Jew aged between twenty and fifty. From Tacitus, we learn that the Judeans were so overwhelmed by their tax burden that they requested imperial relief during the reign of Tiberius (AD 14–37).[6]

* Not surprisingly, the Jerusalem church as the headquarters of the infant Jesus movement supported a proportionately large number of teachers (cf. Acts 6:4; 1 Cor 9:4–6) and felt obliged to provide hospitality for frequent Christian visitors to the Holy City (cf. Rom 12:13; Heb 13:2; 1 Pet 4:9).

E. THE IDENTIFICATION OF "THE POOR"

On only three occasions does Paul refer to the "poor" (*ptōchoi*)— Rom 15:26, 2 Cor 6:10, and Gal 2:10, and in each case, the reference is to economic, not spiritual, poverty.

As Paul depicts the vicissitudes of his ministry in a series of antitheses (2 Cor 6:8–10), he describes himself "as poor but enriching many" (2 Cor 6:10). Though he was merely one person and financially poor, he was able by God's enabling grace to enrich many people spiritually by sharing the good news and all its implications, "the incalculable riches of Christ" (Eph 3:8).

In the other two uses of *ptōchoi*, the article is added and so a class of people is indicated, "the poor." Galatians 2:1–10 recounts the visit of Paul and Barnabas to Jerusalem, at which time they gained from the three "pillars," James, Cephas (= Peter) and John, an endorsement of their mission to the gentiles but also were given a direct request: "All they asked," reports Paul, "was that we should go on remembering [*hina mnēmoneuōmen*, a present tense indicating continual action] the poor—which, in fact [*kai*], was the very thing [*auto touto*] that I had shown my eagerness [*espoudasa*] to do" (Gal 2:10). Here Paul is referring to his prior

6. Tacitus, *Annals* 2.42.

effort with Barnabas in organizing and delivering to Jerusalem the Antiochene famine relief (Acts 11:30; 12:25). He had already met their request once—and unknown to the three, he had already formulated a plan to fulfill their request again (see above, pp. 3–5).

But precisely who were "the poor" that the "pillars" referred to? Some have proposed that because Paul did not say (in Gal 2:10) "go on remembering *their* poor," the reference must be general: "the poor, wherever they may be found," whether inside or outside the Jerusalem church. But (against this view), since both parties in the conversation—the Jerusalem leadership and Paul—knew of the recent relief visit from Antioch to Jerusalem (Acts 11:29–30) and were aware of the current widespread famine that affected Jerusalem in particular (see pp. 10–13), it is highly probable that "the poor" were the needy within the Jerusalem church.

This is confirmed by Paul's statement when he is intimating his intention to visit Jerusalem before continuing on to Rome and Spain (Rom 15:22–29): "Macedonia and Achaia have been pleased to make a contribution for the poor among God's people in Jerusalem" (Rom 15:26). Some scholars translate the crucial phrase, *hoi ptōchoi tōn hagiōn*, as "the poor *who are* God's people" (taking *tōn hagiōn* as an epexegetic/explanatory genitive). Linguistically, this is a possible rendering, but it remains doubtful that Paul would identify the *whole* assembly of believers in Jerusalem as "the poor," conceived of as "the poor in spirit" to whom the kingdom of heaven belongs (Matt 5:3) or that these believers would call themselves "the poor," although at an earlier time the Qumranites called themselves *hā' ebyônîm*, "the poor," and at a later time Jewish Christians who claimed to be successors of the Jerusalem church were called Ebionites (from *'ebyônîm*, "poor ones"). The majority of commentators and English versions rightly take the genitive as *partitive*, "the poor *among* God's people in Jerusalem." These "poor" formed a part of the whole church, a part of an undisclosed size, although presumably a substantial part, including needy widows (Acts 6:1), given the rapid rise in the number of believers (see Acts 2:41, 47; 6:7). The "poverty" referred to is economic (the financially poor; cf. Acts 6:1), not spiritual (the poor in spirit).

Two verses in 2 Cor 8–9 confirm this conclusion. Against the backdrop of Exod 16:18 (the much/little contrasts regarding the gathering of manna) that is quoted in 2 Cor 8:15, the plenty/need contrast of 2 Cor 8:14 must refer to economic plenty and need. Also, 2 Cor 9:12 shows that the immediate function of the collection was to supply "the [physical] necessities of God's people."

It is fair to infer from the expressions "to Jerusalem" and "in Jerusalem" in Rom 15:25–26 that most of the recipients of the relief aid lived in Jerusalem. But just as the earlier financial help was delivered to "the brothers and sisters living in Judea" (= Jerusalem and elsewhere in Judea; Acts 11:29), so this later aid may have been designed not only for poor Jerusalemites within the church but also other indigent believers in Judea. Significantly, 2 Cor 9:13 speaks of the projected Corinthian "generosity in sharing with them [= the needy among God's people; 2 Cor 9:12] and with everyone else in need," presumably whether believer or unbeliever (cf. Acts 20:35; 2 Cor 9:8).

III.

The Contributors to the Collection

A. CHURCHES IN FOUR ROMAN PROVINCES

As we correlate the relevant information from Acts and the Pauline letters, we may assume that contributors to the major relief fund organized by Paul came from churches in four Roman provinces—Galatia, Macedonia, Asia, and Achaia. The church at Rome was not involved because it was not founded by Paul and because it had no knowledge of the monetary fund before his letter to the church there in AD 57 (Rom 15:25–27).

But what do we know about finances in first-century Roman society?

It has been estimated that in Roman society of the first century AD, including the provinces where Paul's churches were situated, 1 percent of the inhabitants were the wealthy elite who controlled most of the city's economic resources(e.g., Erastus, Corinth's "director of public works," Rom 16:23b; see Harris, *Corinth*, 9–10), while 10 percent made up the economic and usually urban "middle class" who often had a surplus beyond living expenses. In this second category were the "householders" such as Lydia (Acts 16:15), Phoebe (Rom 16:1–2), Stephanas (1 Cor 1:16, 16:15),

Chloe (1 Cor 1:11), Gaius (Rom 16:23a), and Onesiphorus (2 Tim 1:16; 4:19), whose "families" may have included slaves (e.g., 1 Cor 7:21–22; 11:21–22) and whose houses may have served as meeting places for believers (e.g., Aquila and Priscilla, 1 Cor 16:19). In the third category, representing roughly 89 percent of a city's inhabitants, were the vast majority of Jesus followers, who may have been employed as unskilled laborers, craft workers, shop assistants, or as a master's slaves. They would be living in residential blocks or in rooms attached to workshops, and generally, they were without income beyond what was essential for living expenses.

As for Corinth in particular, we may assume that apart from Erastus (see above), some Corinthians would fall in the second category above (see 1 Cor 11:21) and so would have some discretionary financial surplus, but doubtless the majority (such as slaves, 1 Cor 7:21–22; 11:22) would fall in the third category and would be able to contribute to the offering only by great sacrifice. What "the present crisis" (1 Cor 7:26) involved, we do not know.

For reasons that are not immediately apparent, in the book of Acts, Luke makes no unambiguous reference to Paul's relief aid project, although there are probable allusions to it in Acts 20:4; 21:17, 20; and 24:17. We stated and answered one explanation in p. 7 above. Another possible explanation is that Luke wished to avoid unnecessarily compromising the reputation of Paul and Christianity in the eyes of Roman authorities by explicitly distinguishing between the half-shekel Temple tax, which was collected and delivered with Roman approval, and the "alms and offerings" (*eleēmosynas . . . kai prosphoras*) that Paul was bringing to Jewish members of the new Israel (cf. "to my nation," Acts 24:17).

B. ACTS 20:4 AND THE DELEGATES

In Acts 20:4, Luke lists the names of seven traveling companions of Paul as he leaves Greece (= Corinth) for Syria and Jerusalem (Acts 20:3, 16). No reason is given why Paul had so many diverse companions for this particular voyage. There is general agreement that while Paul was in Corinth for three months (Acts 20:2–3), he wrote Romans, so that we can identify the projected Jerusalem visit mentioned by Luke with the imminent Jerusalem visit mentioned by Paul in Romans 15:25: "At present . . . I am on my way to Jerusalem to serve [or, with aid for] God's people there." Accordingly, we can deduce that these seven companions of Paul are traveling with him to Jerusalem to deliver the relief aid.

Luke has listed these seven companions according to Roman province:

- Macedonia: Sopater of Berea, Aristarchus, and Secundus of Thessalonica. Luke may have joined these men at Philippi (the second "we" passage begins at Acts 20:5) and may himself have represented the church there.
- Galatia: Gaius of Derbe, Timothy (of Lystra; cf. Acts 16:1–2)
- Asia: Tychicus and Trophimus (of Ephesus; cf. Acts 21:29)

Since we know that certain churches had appointed delegates in connection with the collection (1 Cor 16:3; 2 Cor 8:23), we may legitimately infer that these seven men were representatives of churches from Macedonia, Galatia, and Asia. There is no mention of Galatia and Asia in Rom 15:26 ("Macedonia and Achaia have been pleased to make some contribution for the poor among God's people at Jerusalem") or in 2 Cor 8–9. But this is no evidence that Galatia and Asia failed to contribute. Perhaps Macedonia and Achaia are highlighted because Paul had given special attention to these two provinces.

C. THE INVOLVEMENT OF "ACHAIA"

The term "Achaia" in Rom 15:26 will refer principally to Corinth, but here it will include areas near Corinth such as Cenchreae (Rom 16:1) and possibly even Athens (Acts 17:34). Exactly how the collection progressed at Corinth is uncertain. The Corinthians may have first heard of the project in Paul's nonextant "previous letter" (1 Cor 5:9, 11, written about AD 53) or by visitors from Galatia (cf. 1 Cor 16:1). The "now concerning" of 1 Cor 16:1 (spring AD 55) suggests that the Corinthians had agreed to participate in the relief and had requested directions about it in an earlier letter to Paul. Whatever progress may have been made at Corinth seems to have halted by the time of 2 Corinthians (fall AD 56) (cf. 2 Cor 8:11), owing to (1) Paul's "painful visit" (summer or fall AD 55, 2 Cor 1:23—2:1); (2) an embarrassing incident (2 Cor 2:5–11) involving "the person who did the wrong" and "the injured party" (2 Cor 7:12) and its aftermath; (3) the adverse influence of the intruders from Palestine (2 Cor 11:13–15, 20) who at least for a period were supported by some Corinthian sympathizers (2 Cor 11:7–12); and possibly (4) a rumor or accusation that in orchestrating the collection, Paul was an "unscrupulous trickster," lining his own pockets through his agents, Titus and others (2 Cor 12:16–18).

As for the revival of the collection at Corinth, when Paul sent Titus to deliver and reinforce the effect of the "severe letter" (2 Cor 2:12–13; 7:5–16), he probably encouraged him to revive the flagging collection if the church responded favorably to the letter (cf. 2 Cor 8:6a). Once Titus had reassured Paul of the Corinthians' loyalty to him (2 Cor 7:6–13, 16), Paul was able to press for the speedy completion of the project (2 Cor 8:11). Evidently in the five or so months between the writing of 2 Corinthians (fall AD 56) and Romans (early AD 57), the Corinthians had responded to Paul's urging (Rom 15:26).

But why, then, is there no mention of representation from Corinth in the list of delegates in Acts 20:4, especially in light of 1 Cor 16:3? It is improbable that Paul himself was their appointed delegate, because one reason for his requirement of delegates was to avoid any possible accusation that he had initiated the offering for his own financial gain (2 Cor 8:18–21). Although Titus had been intimately involved with the whole project in Corinth (2 Cor 8:6, 17) and Paul described him as "my partner and coworker among you" (2 Cor 8:23), he is not named as the Corinthian delegate; indeed, he is never mentioned in Acts. Perhaps the list of delegates in Acts 20:4 is incomplete or the gift from Corinth to Jerusalem was sent independently of Paul.

IV.

The Significance of the Collection
for Paul

A ny project undertaken by an individual that demands con-
centrated effort over a prolonged period of time probably
arises from a variety of motives and fulfills several aims. In Paul's
case, his motivations in organizing relief aid for Jerusalem will cor-
respond to his several roles as evangelist, pastor, theologian and
strategist. How seriously he viewed this project may be gauged
from the fact that he was willing to risk his life to ensure its success
(Rom 15:31a; cf. Acts 20:3, 24).

We may conveniently group Paul's motives and aims in de-
signing this relief aid under three broad headings. (The following
is partially dependent on Harris, *2 Cor*, 94–100 and is used with
permission.)

A. HISTORICAL

1. All of Paul's effort in arranging for the collection was a tangible sign of his fulfillment of a promise. As mentioned earlier, on his second post-resurrection visit to Jerusalem with
   the aid from the Antiochene church (Acts 11:29–30; 12:25),

the Jerusalem leadership not only affirmed the legitimacy of Paul's gentile mission (Gal 2:9) but also made a single request: "They asked only one thing—that we should continue to remember [*mnēmoneuōmen*, present continuous action] the poor, which was the very thing I had already shown myself to be eager [*kai espoudasa*] to do" (Gal 2:10). Although the verse does not record Paul's response to the leaders' request, his immediate comment that he had already shown his commitment to "remember the poor" (in arranging and delivering the Antiochene aid) implies his intention to continue this course of action that was undoubtedly expressed in a promise.

2. When Paul finally arrived in Jerusalem in AD 57 with a representative group of his gentile converts—perhaps some eleven years after he contemplated the possibility of a collection for the poor—he was able to introduce these friends to the local congregation as evidence of his faithful performance of the role as apostle to the gentiles that had been entrusted to him by the Jerusalem leadership in AD 46: "They agreed that we should go to the gentiles" (Gal 2:9).

3. The safe delivery of the offering given by the gentiles marked the climax of Paul's ministry in the eastern Mediterranean. He now planned to turn westward for pioneer evangelism in Spain after visiting believers in Rome who could form a support base for the new venture (Rom 15:23–29).

4. It is quite possible that an underlying (and even unconscious) motive in the collection project was the apostle's desire to compensate in part for his earlier systematic persecution of the Jerusalem church. Although his violent repression of Christians extended beyond the frontiers of Israel (Acts 9:2; 26:11, "foreign cities"), his "murderous threats against the Lord's disciples" (Acts 9:1) focused on Jerusalem. Before Herod Agrippa II he confessed that in his "furious rage," he had imprisoned or punished many Jerusalem believers, had cast his vote in favor of their condemnation and death, and

had tried to make them recant by blaspheming Christ (Acts 26:10–11). Imagine Paul's meeting the son or daughter of a parent who had endured a synagogue whipping or had been slain because of his barbarous intervention. Sustained effort in arranging for the relief of the poor in the mother church must have helped to alleviate Paul's acute embarrassment at having been such a vigorous and relentless persecutor (cf. 1 Cor 15:9; Gal 1:13).

B. THEOLOGICAL

1. Above all, this relief mission was seen as an expression of brotherly love (2 Cor 8:8, 24; Rom 12:13, "Share with the Lord's people who are in need"; Rom 13:8, "the continuing debt to love one another"). Such action brings honor to Christ (2 Cor 8:19) and God (2 Cor 9:13) and demonstrates Paul's readiness to help (2 Cor 8:19). For Paul, interchurch social concern operated on the same principle as intrachurch charity—the need to demonstrate the interdependence of members of the body of Christ (1 Cor 12:25–26) by sharing resources (Rom 12:13).

2. Paul viewed the charitable aid he was organizing as more than an endeavor to relieve poverty, for other churches were also facing desperate poverty at the time of the great famine. The Macedonian churches, for example, were grappling with relentless poverty (2 Cor 8:2). This voluntary gift from gentile believers to Jewish believers effectively symbolized both the prior destruction of "the hostile dividing wall" that separated gentile from Jew and also the resultant creation of inviolable unity in Christ (Eph 2:11–22). Three further proposals have been made about Paul's theological motivations for the collection enterprise, but they remain unconvincing.

3. It has been suggested that Paul was fulfilling a solemn obligation imposed by the Jerusalem leaders to recognize the

primacy or spiritual supremacy of the mother church in Jerusalem; Paul was obeying a directive. But we have seen (see A.1 above) that Gal 2:9–10 depicts an amicable "gentlemen's agreement" about joint participation in the task of evangelism and an accompanying desire or wish that Paul (and Barnabas) should continue to remember the poor. No verb of commanding or requiring is expressed. When the three Jerusalem "pillars" spoke to Paul about "remembering the poor," they were not levying a tax or imposing a requirement.

4. Some scholars have proposed that Paul saw the offering as a Christian equivalent of the Jewish Temple tax that was a contribution of a half-shekel (= two Roman dinars) paid annually by every adult male Jew for the maintenance of the Temple in Jerusalem and in particular the offering of the daily public sacrifices for the Jewish nation (cf. Matt 17:24–27). Now there are several similarities between Paul's collection and the temple tax—for example, Jerusalem was the destination; Pentecost was a significant date for the delivery (cf. Acts 20:16); and the contributions were a tangible sign of solidarity and unity (cf. Rom 15:27). And the apostle may have borrowed certain organizational elements from the Temple tax—for example, delegates were appointed from each local community to accompany the funds to Jerusalem (cf. 1 Cor 16:3), and special precautions were taken so that persons involved in handling the funds should be above reproach (cf. 2 Cor 8:20–21). But whereas the Temple tax was a compulsory tax of a specific amount levied on every Jewish male aged twenty or older (Exod 30:14–15) and paid once a year but delivered to Jerusalem three times a year, primarily for the offering of daily sacrifices in the Temple, Paul's collection was a single project involving voluntary gifts of varying amounts (1 Cor 16:2; 2 Cor 8:12), contributed by Jew and gentile, young and old, male and female, at different times in different places, basically for the relief of the material needs of certain individuals within the Jerusalem church.

5. Some have suggested that in Paul's thinking, the conversion of Israel was linked to the success of the collection project. When Paul arrived in Jerusalem with a representative group of believing gentiles, Old Testament prophecies would be fulfilled that predicted that in the last days nations along with their wealth would flow into Jerusalem (Isa 2:2–3; 60:5–6; Mic 4:1–2). This would provoke the Jewish nation to jealousy (Deut 32:21, cited in Rom 10:19) and thus prompt their conversion to Christ (Rom 11:13–15, 25–26).

Against this proposal, two observations are in order.

1. There is no reference to the role of the collection and its delivery to Jerusalem as an "eschatological provocation" in either Rom 9–11 or 2 Cor 8–9, where we would expect the issue to be addressed.

2. Since Paul hoped that after the delivery of the completed collection he would visit Rome and then engage in evangelism in Spain (Rom 15:28), any close link between the gentile gift to Jewish Christians in Jerusalem and the arrival of the end would seem to be compromised.

C. PASTORAL

1. Paul was a strategist as well as a theologian. He envisaged the collection as not only demonstrating but also cementing Jewish-gentile unity. At every stage of his career, Paul was concerned to maintain unity within each local community of Christians (e.g., 1 Cor 1:10; Phil 2:2; Eph 4:3). But he was equally committed to preserving unity among churches, and in particular between the predominantly gentile congregations outside Judea and the Jewish mother church of Jerusalem. Just as gentile converts living in Greco-Roman cities may well have been predisposed to view Jewish Christians in far-off Palestine as rigid conservatives to whom they owed

nothing, so believers in Jerusalem and Judea may have been reluctant to regard gentile Christians as fully accredited citizens of the new Israel. If, however, gentile believers gave generously to the offering for the poor and Jewish Christians received it graciously, the sense of unity would be enhanced. In spite of Paul's undoubted hope that a successful collection would increase unity, he realistically feared that the outcome could lead to disunity. So he urged the Roman Christians to join him in praying that he might be rescued from the unbelieving Jews in Judea and that God's people in Jerusalem would favorably receive the relief aid (Rom 15:31). If his life was threatened by Jewish unbelievers (cf. Acts 20:3, 22–25), Jerusalem Christians might feel compelled to reject the collection, lest by accepting it they might provoke fresh persecution or compromise their witness to fellow Jews.

2. Paul the pastor recognized how appropriate it was to repay indebtedness. The almsgiving shown in the collection dramatized in material terms the spiritual indebtedness of gentile believers to the church in Jerusalem. Paul insisted that "they [gentile believers] are in debt to them [God's people in Jerusalem, Rom 15:26], for if the gentiles have gained a share in their spiritual blessings, they certainly ought [*opheilousin kai*] to be of service to them with regard to material goods" (Rom 15:27). If Jesus could say "salvation comes from the Jews" (John 4:22), Paul can affirm, in effect, "it was ultimately from Jerusalem that the good news reached you gentiles." Just as it is proper and needful for children to honor parents, so it was appropriate and necessary for daughter churches to support the mother church, and this, not as a sign of inferiority but rather of family loyalty.

3. Sadly, disunity was a recurrent problem in the first-century Corinthian church—witness 1 Cor 1:10–17; 11:18, 22 (in AD 55), 2 Cor 11:12–13; 12:20–21 (in AD 56), and 1 Clem. 3:3; 14:2; 51:1 (in AD 95 or 96) (see Harris, *Corinth, passim*). Doubtless Paul will have hoped that Corinthian participation

in a worthy common cause would help to promote unity within the church at Corinth as well as bonding gentile congregations to the Jerusalem church.

PART TWO

A Commentary
on 2 Corinthians 8–9

In sections of this Part Two, I am using material (with permission) found in my two commentaries on 2 Corinthians: *The Second Epistle to the Corinthians* and "2 Corinthians" in *The Expositor's Bible Commentary* (Revised Edition. Volume 11 [Romans—Galatians], ed. Tremper Longman III and David E. Garland [Grand Rapids: Zondervan, 2008] 415–545).

I.

Place of Chapters 8 and 9
in 2 Corinthians

In Rom 15:19, Paul states that he had fully proclaimed the gospel of Christ "from Jerusalem as far around as Illyricum." The phrase "as far . . . as [*mechri*] Illyricum" is inclusive and geographical (not exclusive and metaphorical, "to the far west"). Illyricum was the Roman imperial province bordering on the eastern side of the Adriatic Sea, part of "the regions beyond you [Corinthians]" (2 Cor 10:16). It was during Paul's pastoral and evangelistic work in Macedonia (Acts 20:1–2) and his pioneer evangelism in Illyricum (Rom 15:19) that Paul wrote 2 Corinthians (fall AD 56). Though it was sent to the believers in Corinth as a single letter, it was probably composed in stages, not at a single sitting. On the integrity and dating of the letter, see Harris, *2 Corinthians*, 8–67.

Paul's *general* purpose in writing 2 Corinthians was to promote his converts' "upbuilding" (*oikodomē*) (2 Cor 12:19), to strengthen their individual and corporate faith, involving their "restoration" (*katartisis*) (2 Cor 13:9) to proper relations with God, with himself, and with one another.

The letter falls into three clearly defined sections: apologetic, exhortatory, polemical.

- Chapters 1–7 are Paul's explanation of his conduct and apostolic ministry, with "comfort in the midst of affliction" (1:3–7; 7:4, 7, 13) as the theme, and "I must rejoice" (2:3; 6:10; 7:4, 7, 9, 13, 16) as the tone. His *specific* aim is to express his huge relief at the Corinthians' positive response to his "severe letter" that had been delivered by Titus, his emissary (2:6, 9, 12–14; 7:4–16).

- Chapters 8–9 are Paul's summons to complete the collection, with "generosity in the midst of need" (8:2, 9; 9:5–6, 11–13) as the theme, and "you must finish (your collection)" (8:6, 11; 9:3, 5) as the tone. His *specific* aim is to urge the Corinthians to finish before his arrival what they had earlier commendably begun (8:10–11).

- Chapters 10–13 are Paul's defense of his apostolic authority, with "strength in the midst of weakness" (11:30; 12:9–10; 13:9) as the theme, and "I must boast" (11:16–18, 21, 30; 12:1, 5–6, 9) as the tone. His *specific* aim is have the Corinthians prepare for his imminent visit (12:20–21; 13:2, 10) by self-examination and self-judgment (13:1, 5, 11) so that he could avoid having to exercise discipline on his arrival (10:2, 6, 11; 12:19–21; 13:10).

II.

Various Descriptions of the Collection

Given Paul's recognition of the profound importance of the collection (see pp. 20–26 above), it is not surprising that he uses six different terms and six different phrases to describe the project.

A. WORDS

logeia (1 Cor 16:1–2): "collection," "contribution"

eulogia (2 Cor 9:5, twice): "act/gift of blessing," "generous/willing gift"

charis (2 Cor 8:1, 9; 9:8, 14): "grace"

    (2 Cor 8:4): "privilege," "favor"

    (2 Cor 8:6): "act of grace," "charitable act"

    (2 Cor 8:7): "work of grace," "gift of charity"

    (2 Cor 8:19): "offering," "charitable work," "work of grace"

    (2 Cor 8:16; 9:15): "thanks"

koinōnia (2 Cor 8:4; 9:12–13): "sharing," "taking part," "partnership" *diakonia* (2 Cor 8:4; 9:1, 12–13): "charitable gift," "relief aid," "service"

leitourgia (2 Cor 9:12): "(public) service"

B. PHRASES

Rom 15:26: "[the] contribution . . . for the poor among God's people in Jerusalem"

2 Cor 8:4; 9:1: "the charitable gift/relief aid/service for God's people"

1 Cor 16:1: "the collection/contribution for God's people"

Rom 15:31: "my service for Jerusalem"

1 Cor 16:3: "Your gift for Jerusalem"

Gal 2:10: "remembering the poor"

C. WORDS OR PHRASES ASSOCIATED WITH THE COLLECTION IN 2 COR 8–9 BUT NOT ACTUALLY DESCRIBING IT

"Lavish generosity" (8:20; cf. 8:2; 9:11), "good work" (9:8), "love" (8:7–8, 24), "zeal" (8:7–8), "eagerness" (8:11–12, 19; 9:2), "generosity" (8:2; 9:11, 13), "generosity in sharing" (9:13), "the proof afforded by this service" (9:13), "the charitable gift" (9:12), "the harvest of righteousness" (9:10), "the evidence of love" (8:24; cf. 8:7–8)

III.

Verse-by-Verse Commentary

A. HISTORICAL BACKGROUND

1 Cor 16:1 suggests that the Corinthians already knew of the nature, purpose, and destination of the project—and had agreed to participate in the endeavor. In fact, the introductory "now concerning" (*peri de*) in this verse leads us to assume that inquiry about how to manage the collection was part of the church's earlier letter to the apostle. This same *peri de* occurs in 1 Cor 7:1, 25; 8:1; 12:1; 16:12.

We do not know whether the Corinthians had acted on Paul's very explicit instructions: "On the first day of every week, each one of you should set aside a sum of money in keeping with your income, saving it up" (1 Cor 16:1–2). The situation at Corinth seems to have deteriorated after the receipt of Paul's response to their questions in AD 55, so that any progress on the collection was halted. At some stage, a group of Judaizing intruders arrived from Palestine who called into question Paul's apostolic authority (2 Cor 10:10–11) (they are the "false apostles" of 2 Cor 11:13–15). This prompted Paul to pay a hurried and visit from Ephesus to Corinth and back to Ephesus (what he calls a "sorrowful visit," 2

Cor 2:1; 12:21; 13:2) (summer or fall AD 55). He may have wanted to reinforce his directive about removing the incestuous man from their congregation (1 Cor 5:13) and to prevent any further local undermining of his authority.

Some unknown time after this "painful visit," Paul heard that he or his representative had been publicly defamed at Corinth (2 Cor 2:5). In response, he sent Titus to Corinth with a stern or "severe letter" (no longer extant) (2 Cor 2:3) (spring AD 56), written "out of great distress and anguish of heart" (2 Cor 2:4) to arouse the church there to discipline "the one who committed the offense" (2 Cor 7:12; cf. 2:6) so that he would not have to pay another "painful visit" (2 Cor 2:1) and in order to test the Corinthians' obedience to his authority (2 Cor 2:9). With the overwhelmingly positive response of the Corinthians to this "severe letter," as recounted by Titus (2 Cor 7:6–16), the time was ripe for Paul to issue a compelling appeal to the Corinthians to bring their collection to completion (2 Cor 8:11; 9:3, 5) in a letter delivered again by Titus, who would himself have tried to revive the flagging collection (fall AD 56).

B. COMMENTARY

In the following commentary on these two fundamentally important chapters, we will provide an expanded translation and major and minor headings that summarize the content of the chapters. The expansions are designed to indicate the continuity of Paul's thought and to indicate exegetical preferences where the meaning of the Greek is ambiguous or the terms used call for an explanatory paraphrase (see, for example, *anekdiēgētos* in 9:15). While this commentary moves systematically from verse to verse, it may prove rewarding to read these two chapters rapidly paragraph by paragraph in a modern version so that the train of Paul's thinking becomes clear.

Some of what follows reflects observations made in my two commentaries on 2 Corinthians (one on the NIV translation and the other of 1110 pages on the Greek text), but the expanded translation is new.

Paul's Summons to Complete the Collection (2 Corinthians 8–9)

I. The Need for Generosity (8:1–15)

(a) The Generosity of the Macedonians (8:1–6)

8:1 "Now, my dear brothers and sisters, I would like to draw your attention to God's grace shown among the churches of Macedonia."

There could be no better setting for Paul's appeal to the Corinthians to finalize their contribution to the collection than the immediately preceding 7:6–16, where he praises his converts for their warmly positive reaction to Titus as he delivered the "severe letter": "Your deep sorrow, your ardent concern for me, so that my joy was greater than ever. . . . I am glad that I have confidence in you in every respect" (7:7, 16). Then, with his customary pastoral tact, Paul begins his appeal by highlighting a splendid instance of God's grace in action, not by chiding them for allowing their support to lapse. It is not surprising that he chooses the example of the Macedonians since he is writing from Macedonia (7:5; 9:2–4; cf. Acts 20:1–2). Of special relevance is the present tense (*kauchōmai*) in 9:2: "I have been boasting about it [your eagerness to help] to the Macedonians" (= the churches of Philippi, Thessalonica, and Berea).

God's grace (*charis*) is referred to ten times in these two chapters in six different senses.

1. "Grace," God's unconditional kindness (8:9) or his being able to participate worthily in the collection (8:1; 9:8, 14)

2. "Privilege," the honor of participation (8:4)

3. "Act of grace," the collection as a generous act (8:6)

4. "Grace of giving," the virtuous act of sharing (8:7)

5. "Offering," the collection as an expression of goodwill (8:19)

6. "Thanks," the verbal expression of gratitude for an act of benevolence (8:16; 9:15)

35

This word *charis* that lies at the center of Paul's theology is found at the beginning (8:1) and end (9:14–15) of these two chapters, just as it occurs at or near the beginning and the end of each of his letters, forming the opening chord and dying refrain of every Pauline symphony.

8:2 "They [the Macedonians] were undergoing a severe testing of their faith brought on by hardship. Nevertheless, their exuberant joy, coupled [surprisingly!] with their rock-bottom poverty, has overflowed in lavish generosity."

Paul focuses on two paradoxical contrasts that highlight the Macedonians' example of commendable benevolence: hardship and joy, poverty and generosity. Their poverty no more impeded their generosity than their hardship diminished their joy. This latter paradox is found again in 1 Thess 1:6: "You welcomed the message in the midst of severe suffering with the joy inspired by the Holy Spirit." In the liberal giving by the destitute Macedonians to fellow believers not personally known to them, Paul finds evidence of God's grace (8:1). "Lavish generosity" does not describe the actual size of the Macedonian contribution but the open-hearted attitude these Christians showed in their giving. Without doubt, the radical poverty of these believers gave them a unique empathy with "the poor" in the Jerusalem church (Rom 15:26), just as their suffering gave them a special affinity with the churches of Judea which had also suffered at the hands of their own people (1 Thess 2:14).

8:3 "For they contributed to the offering for the Jerusalem believers, as I can testify, not merely as far as their resources would allow but even beyond, acting on their own initiative."

In verses 3–5, Paul gives fourfold evidence of the Macedonian liberality. (1) Their contribution to the aid project was far more generous than their slender means really permitted them; the size of their offering surpassed all expectations (v. 3a–b). (2) It was without anyone's prompting or pressure that they contributed; given their impecunious state, Paul was apparently reluctant to suggest their involvement (v. 3c). (3) With great insistence they pleaded with Paul for the privilege of being involved in the project (v. 4). (4) They did not limit their contribution to financial aid (v. 5).

8:4 "With urgent appeals they pleaded with us for the privilege of fellowship in this task of bringing relief to God's people in Jerusalem."

The urgent request, perhaps conveyed by the Macedonians Gaius and Aristarchus, Paul's "traveling companions" (Acts 19:29), was for the "privilege of sharing/fellowship" (*koinōnia*) in the relief aid. The allusion is to the brotherhood of all the contributors to the project and to the fellowship between the donors and recipients. As contributors to the offering, the Macedonian churches were giving tangible evidence of their oneness with other contributing gentile churches and with the parent body in Jerusalem.

8:5 "And the extent of their giving was not what we had expected. Rather, they gave themselves to the Lord first and foremost [*prōton*] and also put themselves at our disposal in line with God's will."

What outstripped Paul's expectations was the fact that the Macedonian giving was not restricted to financial aid but included the surrender of their very selves, first of all (*prōton*) by rededicating their lives to the Lord Jesus and also by supporting Paul in his present venture in Macedonia. Both wholehearted devotion to Christ and unswerving commitment to Paul, Christ's ambassador, were in keeping with God's will. Paul must have been pleasantly surprised that the Macedonians had not merely given a monetary contribution but had offered personal assistance with the collection in any way he chose. His appeal to the Macedonian example in verses 1–5 was not designed to embarrass the Corinthians, but that was probably its partial effect: He was about to plead with them to *finish* their collection (vv. 6–7, 11), whereas the Macedonians had implored him to let them *begin* theirs (v. 4)!

8:6 "The result was that we encouraged Titus to bring this gracious work of the collection to a conclusion for you, just as he had already made an auspicious start."

Unlike the Macedonians, the Corinthians were not facing persecution or facing financial hardship. The inference? They ought to be all the more generous in their giving and prompt in completing their offering for Jerusalem! And who better to help them achieve these goals than Titus, who had so recently enjoyed diplomatic success at Corinth when he delivered the "painful/severe letter" (2 Cor 7:5–16, esp. 7:13b, 15), had earlier initiated the collection there (cf. 2 Cor 12:18), and may well have shown himself to be a person of considerable financial acumen (cf. Gal 2:1 = Acts 11:29–30)?

(b) A Plea for Liberal Giving (8:7–12)

8:7 "But since you are rich in spiritual blessings of every kind—in faith, in eloquent speech, in knowledge, in wholehearted enthusiasm and in the love that was generated by our preaching and now is evident in you—you ought now to be equally rich in this grace of generosity."

After identifying five specific areas in which the Corinthians "overflow" or "excel" (*perisseuete*) in spiritual giftedness, Paul encourages comparable excellence or equivalent lavishness in their generosity. Like the Macedonians, they had received evidence of God's grace (*charis*, 2 Cor 8:1)—(1) faith in Christ (cf. Eph 1:15) or faith to work miracles (1 Cor 12:9–10); (2) eloquence in declaring the truth; (3) spiritual perceptiveness; (4) every kind of zeal; and (5) love derived from Paul and now residing in them. Receipt of grace should lead to the grace (*charis*) of giving; grace received should prompt grace given.

8:8 "In saying this I am not issuing a command but seeking evidence of the genuineness of your own love by appealing to the example of the eager cooperation shown by the Macedonian believers."

Although Paul had divinely given apostolic authority (2 Cor 10:8; 13:10), he chose not to issue a directive that he might try to enforce, preferring rather to make a suggestion (2 Cor 8:10) or issue an appeal. He realized that if he resorted to giving commands that might be obeyed mechanically, he would compromise his stress on the voluntary nature of Christian giving (2 Cor 8:3;

9:5, 7), he would be open to the charge of domineering (2 Cor 1:24), and his motivation for arranging the collection and the gift itself might become suspect in the eyes of the Corinthians and the recipients in Jerusalem. In the enthusiastic generosity of the Macedonians, he saw a convenient benchmark for assessing the genuineness of the Corinthian love for himself and for their fellow believers.

8:9 "For you know the example of immeasurable grace shown by our Lord Jesus Christ. Though he was rich in his heavenly glory, for your sake he became poor in his earthly state, in order that you might become rich as a result of his poverty."

As Paul seeks to encourage his Corinthian friends to complete their contribution, he has thus far appealed to the example (8:1–5) and eager cooperation (8:8) of the Macedonians, their own auspicious initial involvement (8:6), and their reputation for spiritual excellence (8:7). Now he turns to the supreme motivation for participation in charitable aid—Christ's selfless and sacrificial giving. Paul regularly buttressed ethical injunctions by doctrine (e.g., Rom 15:2–3; Col 3:9–10).

Using a riches–poverty sequence, the apostle reminds his readers that our Lord Jesus Christ himself chose to exchange his royal status as an eternal inhabitant of heaven for a slave's status as a temporary resident on earth: "Although [*ōn*, concessive participle] rich, he became poor" (*eptōcheusen*, ingressive or constative aorist). This "becoming poor" is probably wider than the Johannine "[the Word] became flesh" (John 1:14) or the Pauline "he emptied himself /made himself nothing" (Phil 2:7) and refers not only to his incarnation but to his incarnation, life, and death viewed in a single glance, "his poverty" or self-impoverishment. The eternal Word surrendered all the insignia of majesty and glory and assumed all the frailty and vicissitudes of the human condition. The Macedonians gave when they were desperately poor (8:2); Christ gave when he was incalculably rich. In their current circumstances the Corinthians would have fallen somewhere between these extremes.

8:10 "On this matter of participation in the collection, I am giving you my considered opinion and advice, for this is your appropriate course to follow. After all, you led the way last year, not only by taking action in giving, but even before that, by wanting to do so."

Advising rather than commanding (cf. 8:8) was Paul's chosen approach in dealing with the Corinthian believers regarding the monetary fund. This was expedient in their case because they enjoyed a distinctive place in the history of the project—they had made a beginning before other contributors in two ways: being the first to start contributing, and before that, being the first to decide to contribute. That decision was made "during the last year," around spring AD 55. Paul is complimenting their unswerving desire to participate in the project.

8:11 "Now, however, finish what you began. This will mean that the completion of the project, using the resources that you have, will match the eagerness of desire that you showed at the outset."

What the Corinthians needed now was an exhortation to finish, not a command to begin. Paul was seeking a correspondence between the completion of their contribution to the project and their original enthusiasm in desiring to participate in it. Completion needed to match intention (Phil 1:6). He was not expecting them to give "beyond their means" (8:3) as the Macedonians had. It was to be "according to your means," "as far as your resources allow" (cf. 8:3; 8:12, "according to whatever one possesses").

8:12 "Where there is such an eagerness to give, God accepts the gift and judges its value on the basis of whatever people have at their disposal, not on the basis of what someone does not have."

There are two bases on which God assesses the acceptability of a gift: the "eager desire" (8:11; cf. 9:2) to give that makes the gift voluntary (9:7) and giving in accordance with one's resources. Paul had already directed the Corinthians to set aside a sum of money regularly, "in keeping with your income" (1 Cor 16:2) or "however one has prospered." This directive for giving reflects God's expectation: give in light of what one possesses at the time. From God's perspective, the "value" of a monetary gift is measured not by the actual amount given but by comparing what is given with the total financial resources of the giver (cf. Mark 12:41–44).

(c) The Aim of Equality (8:13–15)

8:13 "Our aim is not that other people should get relief at the cost of your financial hardship. No, our concern is for the equalizing of provision."

Paul's statement of his positive aim in arranging the collection project—(literally) "it is because of [the need for] equality" (8:13b)—should probably be seen against the backdrop of an actual or possible Corinthian objection to the whole enterprise: "If we give sacrificially, as Paul wants, the Jerusalem poor will be financially comfortable, and we will be economically depressed." From 1 Cor 11:17–22, it is clear that there was tension at Corinth between certain wealthy believers with their "private suppers" and some destitute fellow believers, probably slaves, who were humiliated for being poor.

In responding to such an objection, Paul assures his readers (or hearers) that his aim in the project was simply to pursue equality, that is, to provide sufficient provision for all to afford the necessities of life. He would have been well aware of the elevation of "equality" or "fair dealing" (*isotēs*) in Greek thought as a cardinal virtue in law, political theory, and even interpersonal relationships. How much more between those who are one in Christ!

8:14 "In the present circumstances you have a surplus of resources that can be applied to their deficiency of resources, so that on some future occasion their surplus will in turn serve to supply your deficiency. The purpose is equality of provision."

Corinth was renowned for its pursuit of wealth that was readily available to those committed to personal enterprise and hard work. The city was well known for its successful tourism, its flourishing pottery and ceramics industry, and its skilled labor for the building and maintenance of ships. As a result of his observation or experience, Paul knew that many of the Corinthians had some disposable income, money available to them on a regular basis that was above what they needed for essentials. He had previously given them directions: "On the first day of every week, each of you should set aside and save whatever extra money you earn" (1 Cor 16:2). It was this "surplus" (*perisseuma*), accumulated in weekly installments, that would meet the "deficiency" or "shortage" or "shortfall" (*hysterēma*) of God's people in Jerusalem (cf. 9:12).

The ongoing economic need in Jerusalem has been discussed above (pp. 11–13). Paul is not now predicting some future economic dearth in Corinth and prosperity in Jerusalem, some grand reversal of the present "surplus–deficiency" situation. It is the principle of reciprocal sharing ("equality of provision") that he is defending.

8:15 "This point is made in the scriptural account of the manna. 'The person who gathered much did not have anything left over, and the person who gathered only a little did not have any shortage.'"

Paul now illustrates the equalization of provision (8:14) by the well-known wilderness experience of the Israelites (Exod 16:11–36) when God provided them with quail in the morning and "thin flakes like frost" (= manna) in the evening. People were directed to gather an *omer* each (about 2.3 liters) before it melted, to eat it on the day it was gathered, and to gather a double measure on the sixth day. During the process of measuring the collected manna, there was a miraculous equalizing of supply to one *omer* each, so that "the person who gathered much had no surplus, and the person who gathered little had no deficiency" (Exod 16:18). By God's intervention, inequalities were eliminated. But there were basic differences between Israelite and Christian experience: The equality in the wilderness resulted from a divine miracle and was enforced and inescapable; the equality in the church would result from human initiative and would be voluntary and so not automatic.

II. The Mission of Titus and His Companions (8:16–9:5)

(a) The Delegates and Their Credentials (8:16–24)

8:16 "I am grateful to God for putting into the heart of Titus the same eagerness for your welfare as I have."

Titus's "eagerness," like the Israelites' manna, was supplied by God, and it was comparable to Paul's own enthusiasm for the Corinthians' highest spiritual good—not for their money (cf. 12:14, "What I want is not your possessions but you"). Paul's outburst of gratitude for God's gracious intervention ("Thanks be to God") occurs three times in 2 Corinthians (2:14; 8:16; 9:15).

8:17 "Evidence of this eagerness may be found in his ready consent to my appeal. What is more, because he is very eager to help, he is setting off to visit you on his own initiative."

This evidence was twofold. First, Titus welcomed Paul's request that he should return to Corinth to help to finalize the collection there. Second, there is his wholehearted decision to return to Corinth, without any pressure from Paul. How could Titus accede to Paul's request and yet act "on his own accord"? Perhaps Paul is saying his request turned out to be superfluous, for Titus was already keen to go to Corinth.

8:18 "And we are sending as his colleague the well-known brother whose service for the gospel is praised throughout all the churches."

Here the term "brother" (*adelphos*) signifies not only a fellow believer in God's family but also a colleague in Christian work, perhaps as an evangelist or teacher or administrator (cf. 1 Cor 12:28). He had been appointed "by the churches" (8:19) and was highly respected "throughout all the churches," which may be restricted to the Macedonian churches but may include "all the churches" of the Pauline mission (as in 1 Cor 7:17; 2 Cor 11:28) or all Christian churches in general.

But why does Paul not name this "brother" and the one mentioned in 8:22? He could be pointing to the primacy of Titus in the delegation, but more probably, the Corinthians had not met these two "brothers" who would be introduced to the church by Titus.

8:19 "But not only does he have a fine reputation. These churches have appointed him to be our traveling companion and helper in connection with this benevolent gift that is being administered by us to promote the glory of the Lord himself and to demonstrate our eager readiness to help our fellow believers."

This brother had been selected and commissioned by the churches to travel with Paul as his assistant (*synekdēmos*) in administering the collection and conveying it to Jerusalem. In the final analysis, Paul himself (*huph' hēmōn*, "by us") was the sole administrator of the project, responsible for its genesis, its organization, its completion, and its safe delivery to Jerusalem. His twofold and coordinate aim in organizing the charitable aid is expressed by a single preposition: "for the purpose of" (*pros*), primarily "to enhance the glory of the Lord God himself" (not Paul) since the success of the project would prompt people to praise God (9:11–13); and secondarily "to show [for all to see] his goodwill" toward the mother church of Christendom. A similar dual pattern is found in 9:12: "The carrying out of this act of service is not only supplying the needs of God's people [in Jerusalem], but is also overflowing in many expressions of thanks to God."

8:20 "In acting this way we are taking every precaution to ensure that no one will have any reason to find fault with us in the way we handle this lavish gift."

As a strong defender of his own financial independence (1 Cor 9:12b, 15, 18; 2 Cor 11:9–12), Paul was particularly susceptible to a malicious charge of embezzlement regarding the collection—such as a charge from one of his detractors at Corinth (cf. 2 Cor 2:17; 7:2; 11:7–9; 12:14–18). One reason for his requirement that churches appoint delegates (cf. Acts 20:4) and for his appointment and sending of these three accredited envoys to Corinth (8:16–23) before he himself arrived (9:5) was to prevent any grounds for suspicion of the way he handled this sizeable relief fund. He was vigorously protective of his financial integrity. Unlike Ananias before him (Acts 5:1–3), he was not quietly "keeping back" part of the fund for his private use.

8:21 "For we are making careful prior arrangements to do what is right and honorable, not simply in the Lord's eyes but also in the eyes of people."

Paul now restates in positive terms what he had expressed negatively in the previous verse. Alluding to Prov 3:4, he affirms that careful forethought is needed so that in both divine and human eyes he is seen to be acting rightly and honorably, as well as to avoid censure. Since he was conducting the whole project "for the Lord's glory" (8:19) and for human benefit (8:4; 9:1), it was appropriate for him to take precautionary measures on both fronts.

8:22 "Moreover, along with Titus and the brother just mentioned we are sending another Christian brother of ours. He is someone whose earnest devotion we have been able to test and prove in many circumstances and on many occasions. In the present matter that earnestness of his is all the stronger, owing to the total confidence that he has in you."

The second anonymous companion of Titus is now introduced and his credentials given. He had already often emerged from testing as a brother of renowned devotion. His proven enthusiasm in many settings was all the more intense because of his profound confidence in the Corinthians—that may have resulted from an earlier visit to Corinth or from conversations with Titus (cf. 7:7, 11, 13b–15) or with Paul, who had recently been applauding the Corinthians to the Macedonians (9:2).

8:23 "If questions are raised about the credentials of Titus, remember that he is a partner of mine who has shared in my labors for you. If questions are raised about the two brothers we are sending with Titus, know that they are delegates of the Macedonian churches and each of them is a trophy of Christ's grace."

In this summary recommendation of all three delegates, Titus stands first, as in 8:16–22, for he was Paul's appointee and leader of the delegation, being Paul's personal associate (*koinōnos emos*) and coworker with regard to the Corinthians, whereas Titus's two companions were sent by Paul (8:18, 22) but appointed by the Macedonian churches (8:19, 23b). Significantly, it was believers from Macedonia who had offered Paul their support and services for the collection enterprise (8:5). These two delegates are said to be "the glory [*doxa*] of Christ" in that they were "people in whom Christ is glorified" or "a credit to Christ" or "trophies of God's saving grace."

8:24 "So then, give these men visible and clear proof that your Christian love is genuine and that my taking pride in you was justified, so that the churches they represent can see your fine Christian conduct."

This final appeal is based on (*oun*, "so then") the whole preceding "letter of commendation" (8:16–23). The Corinthians were to give tangible proof of their genuine love, presumably love for the delegates, for Paul, for Christ, and for the indigent members of the Jerusalem church. Also they are encouraged to give outward evidence of the truth of Paul's confident boasting about their love and their commitment to the collection project as shown by their readiness to help (9:2; cf. 7:14; 8:10–11). This proof would be clearly shown, we may assume, if the Corinthians received the delegates warmly, offered them hospitality, and cooperated with their suggestions about how to complete their contribution to the monetary fund.

(b) The Need for Readiness (9:1–5)

9:1 "With regard to this charitable service for God's people, there is no need for me to write further."

After saying "there is no need for me to write further," Paul proceeds to speak further (in 9:2–15) about this charitable project! This rhetorical device, known as *paraleipsis* ("a passing over" of a prior statement), also occurs in Heb 11:32–38.

9:2 "For I know how willing and eager you are to help. Indeed, I have been taking pride in telling the Macedonians here about this on your behalf, reporting that you in Achaia have been standing ready to give since last year. As a result, the persuasive example of your enthusiasm has stirred the majority of them into action."

Since Paul knew that the Corinthians had shown an "eager willingness" (*prothymia*) to take part in the collection, he was able to appeal to their "readiness" of desire or intention and their enthusiasm (*zēlos*) when encouraging the Macedonians to continue with their own collection. His appeal proved successful, for the majority of Macedonians were spurred on to imitate the Corinthians' enthusiasm and advance their own liberal giving (8:1–5, 8). "The majority" implies a minority—perhaps those who had already supported Paul financially (2 Cor 11:8–9) and felt they were unable to do more, or some who were so poverty-stricken (cf. 2 Cor 8:2) that they were unable to contribute at the time but planned to do so when their circumstances changed. "Achaia" may refer to all the Christians in the Roman province of Achaia, including the Corinthian believers, or may stand for "Corinth" in a flattering identification of the province with the city.

9:3 "But I am sending Titus and the two church delegates to ensure that my pride in your eagerness and readiness may not prove to be empty words in this matter and also to ensure that you are in fact fully ready, just as I was assuring them you would be."

Two reasons are given for Paul's sending of the three brothers to Corinth: to prevent his boasting to the brothers about the Corinthians (2 Cor 8:24) from turning out to be unjustified, and to make sure the Corinthians were in a state of full readiness with regard to their contribution to the collection when he arrived. A distinction must be drawn between two types of "readiness." In verse 2, the readiness was a matter of preparedness of intention (cf. 2 Cor 8:10–11). Here it is a case of preparedness of completion.

9:4 "Otherwise, if some Macedonians were to come with me on my visit to you and find your collection not complete, we would perhaps be embarrassed and ashamed—to say nothing of your shame—for being so confident about you."

Here Paul gives a second negative reason (see 9:3) for his dispatch of the three emissaries to Corinth: his concern about mutual humiliation if the Corinthians should be discovered to be still unprepared when he arrived. He may really want to say "lest . . . you perhaps be humiliated," but to avoid offending anyone, he applies the point primarily to himself with the ostensible afterthought being all the more potent for being parenthetical. The "some Macedonians" are not the two unnamed brothers of 8:18–23 but probably the bearers of the Macedonian collection (cf. 8:5).

9:5 "So to avoid mutual humiliation I have thought it necessary to urge these three brothers to visit you before I come and to organize the completion of this gift of blessing before my arrival—a gift that you have already promised. I want it to be ready as a generous gift and not as a gift that is given grudgingly."

This threesome formed an advance party to Corinth, not only to deliver and explain the present letter (the canonical 2 Corinthians) but also to facilitate the completion of the collection there, given the Corinthian lack of organizational skills (cf. 1 Cor 14:33, 40). Paul here describes the Corinthian love-gift as a "gift of blessing" (*eulogia*) because it would be a blessing to the destitute believers in Jerusalem (9:12), would prompt the Jerusalemites to praise God (9:11–13), and would lead to God's gracious blessing on their own lives (9:8–10). Presumably, they had pledged their support in the letter they sent Paul (perhaps in early AD 55) that asked for advice about the collection (cf. 1 Cor 16:1). He wanted their promised gift to be generous, not "a gift that reflects avarice" (*pleonexia*), that is, a scanty contribution that is given grudgingly. The skillful work of the delegates among the Corinthian congregation would be a protection against "last-minute" giving that would probably result in a minimal gift parted with reluctantly.

III. The Resources and Results of Generosity (9:6–15)

With his reference to the completion of the Corinthian collection in 9:5 (cf. 8:11), Paul has from one perspective reached the climax of chapters 8 and 9, with the remainder of chapter 9 simply reviewing the resources and results of their anticipated generous giving.

(a) God's Enrichment of the Giver (9:6–11)

9:6 "What I am saying is summed up in the farming axiom: If you sow sparingly, you will also reap a meager harvest; but if you sow liberally, you will also reap a bountiful harvest."

To emphasize the rewards of generous giving (9:5), Paul quotes what appears to be a proverb: "Scanty sowing, scanty harvest; plentiful sowing, plentiful harvest" (TCNT). No precise parallel is known, but compare Prov 11:24–25; 19:17; 22:8–9; Luke 6:38; Gal 6:7. Paul's point is the correspondence between the quantity of the seed sown and the quantity of the harvest. He is implying that a meager contribution from the Corinthians would produce some harvest, but his wish was for a substantial gift that would produce a correspondingly sizeable harvest of benefits for both givers and recipients.

9:7 "I want each of you to give just what you have already resolved in your mind to give. Do not give regretfully, as though giving involved a painful loss, nor under pressure, as though giving were compulsory. God loves and prospers the person who gives cheerfully."

Just as the sower is free to plant as much seed as they choose—whether sparingly or generously (9:6)—so each giver should make their own decision exactly how much to give so as to avoid impulsive or casual giving. Also, giving regretfully or under constraint must be avoided, for God takes special pleasure in the type of giving—cheerful giving—that reflects his own manner of giving (cf. Heb 13:16).

The contemporary analogy for this Jerusalem collection was not the obligatory annual temple tax that was levied on all adult male Jews but the voluntary offerings that Jews, proselytes, and even gentiles made in Jerusalem.

9:8 "Indeed, God is fully able to shower you with every kind of blessing in plentiful measure, so that in all circumstances and at all times you may have total sufficiency for your own needs and at the same time abundant means to carry out good work of every kind."

Verses 8–14 are a commentary on the concept of "reaping bountifully" (8:6b), indicating the benefits that come to the giver if the principles of giving stated in 8:6b–7 are followed. "Every kind of blessing" (*pasa charis*), material and spiritual, is a God-ordained outcome for generous and cheerful giving. This divine blessing is designed to promote not passive ease but active benevolence ("good work of every kind"). For Paul, "sufficiency" or "contentment" (*autarkeia*) was not, as in Greek philosophy, the self-sufficiency and contentment of the individual who was self-supporting and independent of other people and of circumstances. It was "God-sufficiency," a complete dependence on God's ability to create the desire to give, to supply plentiful resources to give to others, and to grant contentment with one's own possessions and situation in life (cf. Phil 4:11–13; 1 Tim 6:6).

9:9 "As Scripture says about the generous person:

> "They scattered his gifts far and wide; they freely gave to the needy.
> Their kind deeds will continue as long as they live."

Some argue that the implied subject of this verse from Psalm 112:9 is God. But in the context the subject is more probably God-fearers (who are the subject in Ps 112; see v. 1) or (better) generous Corinthian contributors. In that case, "their righteousness" refers to their kind deeds or benevolence to the needy or poor that will remain a way of life, not isolated or irregular action, because God constantly supplies them with the resources to give (9:8, 10).

9:10 "God is the one who bountifully provides seed for people to sow and thus bread for them to eat, so he will certainly provide and multiply seed for you to sow and he also will increase the harvest produced by your kind deeds."

Verse 10 reiterates and expands verse 8, both verses affording a ringing assurance of God's bountiful provision that makes possible generous actions of every sort. Since Paul knew that the God of nature is also the God of salvation, his thought naturally moves from God's generous provision in nature to his certain provision—and multiplication!—of full resources that will enable the Corinthians to "sow generously." The first reference to "seed" is literal, the second is figurative.

9:11 "Then you will be enriched by God in every way, enabling you to show all kinds of generosity which will produce a harvest of thanksgiving to God as we pass on your gift for your fellow believers."

This verse is transitional. The first part summarizes 9:8, the prior generosity of God. The second announces the main theme of 9:12–15, the offering of thanksgiving to God that would be occasioned by the generosity of the Corinthians. The divine beneficence is designed not to facilitate the accumulation of wealth but to make possible all kinds of liberality. This verse encapsulates Paul's emphasis on the priority and finality of God in Christian stewardship. God enriches the Corinthians, who then give generously so that the beneficiaries give thanks to God. "From him and . . . for him are all things" (Rom 11:36).

(b) The Offering of Prayer to God (9:12–15)

9:12 "For when you perform this act of public service, you are not merely meeting the needs of God's people. In addition, your giving will produce a flood of thanksgiving to God."

In Classical Greek the term *leitourgia* denoted "public service" carried out by private citizens at their own expense. In the LXX it became a technical term for priestly service in the temple (e.g., 2 Chron 35:16, LXX). So it could refer to "public service" performed for the benefit of a community, or religious service, "holy service" or "service" in a non-technical, popular sense. Here the phrase "the performance of this act of public service" refers to the carrying out of the collection project as a whole, a distinctive act of community assistance (cf. this technical term in Phil 2:17, 30), but with special reference to the role of Corinthians and other contributors rather than to the distinctive role of Paul or of the Corinthians alone.

But Paul did not place these two stated purposes of the collection—human relief and praise of God—on an equal footing, with the first, historical purpose subsidiary to the second, theological aim. Human philanthropy was less important than praising or glorifying God (9:13), which for Paul was always the highest good and ultimate goal (Rom 15:7; 1 Cor 10:31; Eph 1:12, 14; Phil 2:11).

9:13 "Indeed, this service of giving will provide such evidence of your love and faith that people will glorify God for two things—for your obedience that arises from your allegiance to the gospel of Christ; and for your generosity in sharing your material resources with those in Jerusalem and with everyone in need."

Believers in Jerusalem as well as other Christians (= "people") who had heard of the collection would recognize it as an act of Christian service that proved the reality of the Corinthians' love and the vigor of their faith. Consequently, they would praise and honor God for two reasons. The first reason was the Corinthian obedience to the dictates of the gospel that was prompted by their adherence to the gospel of Christ, a gospel that demands that believers should help to relieve need both inside and outside the family of believers (Rom 12:13; Gal 6:9–10; 1 Tim 6:18). Confessing allegiance to the gospel involves obedience to its requirements.

The second reason to glorify God was the Corinthians' sacrificial liberality (*haplotēs*, "generosity") demonstrated in supplying aid to the needy in Jerusalem and elsewhere. Compare Galatians 6:10: "As we have opportunity, let us do good to all people, especially to those who belong to the family of faith."

9:14 "What is more, as your fellow believers pray for you, their hearts will be drawn to you in love because God's grace rests on you in such unbounded measure."

Having described the response to God of the recipients of the collection in Jerusalem—offering him thanks (9:12)—Paul now focuses on the response of these beneficiaries to their donors in Corinth: They will pray for them and lovingly yearn to verify and applaud in person the extraordinary evidence of God's grace in their lives. What had been true of the Macedonians (8:1) would also be true of the Corinthians; they would be recipients of God's grace that inspired generous giving (cf. 9:6–8).

How could Paul speak so confidently of these outcomes when three or four months later he issues an urgent call to the Christians in Rome to pray that he may be kept safe from the unbelievers in Judea and that the contribution he takes to Jerusalem "may be favorably received by God's people there" (Rom 15:30–31)?

1. Paul believes that "God is able" (9:8) to produce the positive outcomes he has mentioned.

2. By assuming that the Corinthians will contribute generously, he is actually encouraging their participation and precipitating their eager involvement.

3. The concern expressed in Rom 15:31 may be the result of news he had received after the present letter had been sent. Perhaps some Jerusalemite believers had been adversely affected by "the unbelievers in Judea."

4. As it turned out, the leaders in Jerusalem, representing the whole church there, "warmly welcomed" Paul and the delegates on their arrival in Jerusalem with the relief aid (Acts 21:17–20) (see further I.D above).

9:15 "May God be praised for his gift that no words can exhaustively describe!"

Having just spoken of praising God for generous giving between humans (9:13–14), Paul now admonishes all humans to render thanks to God for *his* supremely generous gift. The colorful adjective *anekdiēgētos*, not found in the Greek OT (LXX) or in Greek writers before the Christian era, means "not (*a-*) able to be described (cf. *diēgeomai*, 'describe'; *ekdiēgeomai*, 'tell in detail') exhaustively (*-ek-*)," and cannot be adequately rendered by a single English word such as "inexpressible" or "indescribable" or even by the phrase "beyond description." God's gift is a gift that no words can exhaustively describe. The gift is the salvation Christ brings (Rom 8:32) or, better, Christ himself.

PART THREE

The Relevance of Paul's Collection
for Christian Stewardship

Although two millennia separate Paul's innovative first-century philanthropy from our modern efforts in altruism, what we have in common is the same supreme Lord and Master whose expectations of his stewards remain unchanged. It is these timeless expectations that will be the focus of this Part Three.

I.

The Supreme Lordship of God and Christ

OT: "The Lord—the Lord of all the earth" (Jos 3:13)

"Lord, the Lord Almighty" (Ps 69:6; Isa 6:3)
"Great is our Lord and mighty in power" (Ps 147:5)

NT: "Jesus Christ, who is Lord of all" (Acts 10:36)

"There is but one Lord, Jesus Christ" (1 Cor 8:6)
"You received Christ Jesus as Lord" (Col 2:6; cf. 2 Cor 4:5; 1 Pet 3:15)
"Jesus is Lord" (Rom 10:9; 1 Cor 12:3)

In the New Testament and in the Greek version of the OT (the Septuagint), the word translated as "Lord" or "Master" is *kyrios*, a term that has two basic general senses. A "lord" or "master" may be:

- an owner of items over which they have control, such as a vineyard (Matt 20:8; 21:40) or a harvest (Matt 9:38) or a slave (Luke 12:46) or a donkey (Luke 19:33);

- someone in authority, such as a ruler (Matt 27:63; Acts 25:26) or someone who is respected (John 12:21; Acts 16:30).

Biblical statements about the believer's relationship to God as
Lord or Master fall into two main categories, represented by two
Greek words and two verses from 1 Peter.

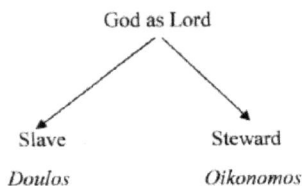

God as Lord

Slave   Steward

Doulos   *Oikonomos*

1. *Doulos*, "slave"

> Live as free people, but do not use your freedom as a
> cover-up for evil; *live as God's slaves.* (1 Pet 2:16)

A slave is someone who belongs wholly to their master and carries
out all his wishes.

Submission and obedience are the slave's hallmark.

In an earlier book of 220 pages, I discussed the implications
of being the slave of God or Christ (*Slave of Christ: A New Testament Metaphor for Total Devotion to Christ*).

It is profoundly significant that the early church's two most
prominent leaders—Peter and Paul—both chose to introduce
themselves as "a slave of Christ Jesus/Jesus Christ" (see 2 Pet 1:1;
Rom 1:1), as did two of Jesus's half-brothers, James and Jude (see
Jas 1:1; Jude 1). The word order in these passages suggests that it
is a higher privilege to be the slave of Christ than to be his apostle
or his brother.

2. *Oikonomos*, "steward"

> Each of you should use whatever gift you have received
> to serve others, as *faithful stewards of God's grace* in its
> various forms. (1 Pet 4:10)

A steward is someone who administers resources entrusted to them by the master for the master's benefit. They may serve as the manager of servants (Luke 12:42), a manager of a master's household (Titus 1:7) and possessions (Luke 16:1, 3, 8), a trustee of an estate (Gal 4:2), an administrator of spiritual treasures (1 Cor 4:1; 1 Pet 4:10), or even a public treasurer or director of public works (Rom 16:23). The OT character Joseph is a prime example of a reliable steward. Potiphar, one of Pharaoh's officials, "put him [Joseph] in charge of his own household, and he entrusted to his care everything he owned . . . ; with Joseph in charge, he did not concern himself with anything except the food he ate" (Gen 39:4, 6).

Faithfulness and creativity are the steward's hallmark.

II.

Christian Stewardship

In this section I am citing passages from 2 Cor 8 and 9, wherever relevant, since I have already (in Part Two) examined these two crucially important chapters verse by verse. There I provided an expanded rendering of each verse; here a more traditional translation will be given. Rather than simply listing passages that illustrate various points (as earlier in the book), I will here cite many of the relevant texts in full so that the potency of the authoritative biblical text will be felt and appreciated. The outlines used and some of the content are based on my earlier brief article on stewardship (*Interest* magazine, February 1979, 4–5).

A. THE NATURE OF STEWARDSHIP

In essence, stewardship is the generous and beneficial use of God-given gifts.

- "Freely you have received; freely give" (Matt 10:8).
- "Each of you should use whatever gift you have received to serve others" (1 Pet 4:10).

Before we can give, we must possess, and before we possess, we must receive. The steward needs an open hand to receive from God and then an active hand to give to others for the glory of God.

God's freely given gifts include creation, physical life, new spiritual life in Christ through the Holy Spirit, distinctive personal talents and the time to develop and use them, and economic resources that may benefit one's physical and spiritual relatives as well as people in general.

- "This is how you ought to regard us: as servants of Christ and stewards [*oikonomous*] of the mysteries God has revealed. Moreover, it is required of stewards [*oikonomois*] that they prove trustworthy" (1 Cor 4:1–2).

- "Now to each person a gift that manifests the Spirit is given for the common good" (1 Cor 12:7).

- "This brother was also chosen by the churches to accompany us while we are administering this generous undertaking in order to honor the Lord himself and to show our eagerness to help" (2 Cor 8:19).

Stewardship is an act of worship and of Christian fellowship. When Christians act as responsible stewards in surrendering themselves and all their talents to God and in sharing God's gifts with others, they are offering to God an acceptable sacrifice.

- "Cornelius stared at him [an angel of God] in fear. 'What is it, Lord?' he asked. The angel answered, 'Your prayers and gifts to the poor have come up as a memorial offering before God'" (Acts 10:4).

- "I urge you, brothers and sisters, in view of God's mercy, to present your bodies as a living sacrifice, holy and acceptable to God—this is your thoughtful service" (Rom 12:1).

- "This service that you perform is not only supplying the needs of God's people but is also overflowing in many expressions of thanks to God" (2 Cor 9:12).

- "Do not neglect to do good and to share what you have, for such sacrifices are pleasing to God" (Heb 13:16).

To be a steward is to be someone who receives and expresses God's grace and demonstrates devotion to Christ.

- "We want you to know, brothers and sisters, about the grace of God that has been granted to the Macedonian churches. In the midst of a very severe ordeal, their exuberant joy and their extreme poverty have overflowed in rich generosity" (2 Cor 8:1–2).

- "They urgently pleaded with us for the privilege of sharing in this service to God's people. They exceeded our expectations in that they gave themselves first of all to the Lord, and then by the will of God also to us" (2 Cor 8:4–5).

- "Since you excel in everything . . . make sure that you also excel in this grace of giving" (2 Cor 8:7).

B. THE EXTENT OF STEWARDSHIP

No Christian is exempt from the obligation to give, since all are beneficiaries of God's generosity. All of life, with its limitless potential, is a trusteeship given to us by God. Stewardship involves more than our material possessions. The breath of life, the opportunities to worship and serve brought by each new day, our family and business relationships, and the knowledge that we acquire are all aspects of our stewardship.

- "What do you have that you did not receive? And if you did receive it, why do you boast as though it were not a gift?" (1 Cor 4:7)

Every Christian is a steward—whether male or female, whether young or old, whether rich or poor. Paul seems to regard "the rich" (1 Tim 6:17) as all those who have more than the bare necessities of life—more, that is, than food, clothing, and shelter (1 Tim 6:8). No believer is denied the privilege of being the Master's steward, as the following passages illustrate.

- "In Joppa there was a disciple named Tabitha [in Greek her name is Dorcas]. She was devoted to good works and acts of charity" (Acts 9:36).

- "Brothers and sisters . . . share with God's people who are in need. Practice hospitality" (Rom 12:1, 13).

- "I ask you to welcome her [our sister Phoebe, Rom 16:1] in the Lord in a way fitting for God's people and give her whatever help she may need from you, for she has been a benefactor on many people and of myself as well" (Rom 16:2).

- "As servants of God we commend ourselves in every way: . . . as sorrowful, yet always rejoicing; as poor, yet making many rich; as having nothing, and yet possessing everything" (2 Cor 6:4, 10).

- "Let a widow be put on the list . . . if she is well attested for her good deeds, such as bringing up children, showing hospitality, washing the feet of God's people, helping those in trouble and devoting herself to good deeds of every kind" (1 Tim 5:9–10).

- "Command those who are rich in this present age not to be arrogant nor to put their hope in wealth, which is so uncertain, but to put their hope in God who richly provides us with everything for our enjoyment. They are to do good, to be rich in good deeds, to be generous and willing to share. In this way they will store up treasure for themselves as a firm foundation for the future, so that they may take hold of the life that really is life" (1 Tim 6:17–19).

- "If anyone has worldly goods and sees a brother or sister in need but shows no pity for them, how can the love of God be in that person?" (1 John 3:17).

C. THE MOTIVATION FOR STEWARDSHIP

The steward's attitude in using the Master's resources is all-important, for this determines whether or not their action gains the Master's approval.

- "If I give away all my possessions and surrender my body to hardship so that I may boast, but do not have love, I gain nothing" (1 Cor 13:3).

- "Because of his faith Abel offered to God a more acceptable sacrifice than Cain's. Through this faith he received approval as a righteous man, when God himself gave approval of his offerings" (Heb 11:4; cf. Gen 4:1–7).

- "Dear children, let us love, not with words or speech, but with actions and in truth" (1 John 3:18).

Stewards follow the example of Christ's self-giving love in gratitude to him.

- "Christ's love compels us" (2 Cor 5:14).

- "You know the generous act of our Lord Jesus Christ, that though he was rich, yet for your sake he became poor, so that by his poverty you might become rich" (2 Cor 8:9).

- "Thanks be to God for his gift that defies adequate description!" (2 Cor 9:15).

- "My command is this: Love one another as I have loved you" (John 15:12).

Stewards are ultimately accountable to the Master for their handling of his resources, and he assumes they have been creative, honest, and reliable.

- "Jesus told his disciples: 'There was a rich man whose manager [*oikonomon*] was accused of squandering his property. So he summoned him and asked him, "What is this I hear about you? Give me an accounting of your management [*oikonomias*], because you cannot be my manager [*oikonomein*] any longer"'" (Luke 16:1–2).

- "It is required of stewards [*oikonomois*] that they prove trustworthy" (1 Cor 4:2).

- "We must all appear before the judgment seat of Christ so that each of us may receive recompense for what has been done while in the body, whether good or evil" (2 Cor 5:10).

Stewards aim to achieve (on a small scale) equality in the provision of the necessities of life.

- "Our desire is not that there should be relief for others and pressure on you, but that there might be equality. At the present time your plenty will supply their need, so that in turn their plenty will supply your need. The goal is equality" (2 Cor 8:13–14). (See the commentary on these verses in Part Two above [cf. Deut 15:7–8].)

Stewards should aim to repay spiritual debts in material terms.

- "Macedonia and Achaia have been pleased to share their resources with the poor among God's people in Jerusalem. They were pleased to do it, and indeed they owe it to them. For if the gentiles have come to share in the Jews' spiritual blessings, they ought in turn to share their material blessings with the Jews" (Rom 15:26–27).

- "The person who receives instruction in the word of God should share all good things with their instructor" (Gal 6:6).

- "The elders who govern well are worthy of double honor, especially those who toil in preaching and teaching. For Scripture says, 'Do not muzzle an ox while it is treading out the grain,' and 'The worker deserves his wages'" (1 Tim 5:17–18).

D. THE EXERCISE OF STEWARDSHIP

To indicate how stewardship should be exercised, we will indulge in a series of antitheses that will highlight the proper and improper attitudes or courses of action.

1. Voluntary, not enforced. Regarding the collection, Paul says "I am not commanding you" (2 Cor 8:8) and "I am simply giving you my advice" (2 Cor 8:10).

   - "I can testify that they [the Macedonians] *voluntarily gave* according to their means, and even beyond their means" (2 Cor 8:3).

   - "Each of you should give *what you have made up your mind to give*, not reluctantly or under compulsion, for God loves a cheerful giver" (2 Cor 9:7; cf. Exod 25:1–2).

2. Generous, not parsimonious. One of the most common causes of spiritual barrenness is a failure to be liberal in giving.

   - "In the midst of a very severe ordeal their [the Macedonians'] exuberant joy and their extreme poverty have overflowed in *rich generosity*" (2 Cor 8:2).

   - "Remember this: Whoever sows sparingly will also reap sparingly, *and whoever sows generously will also reap generously*" (2 Cor 9:6).

   - "Command them [those who are rich in this present world] to do good, to be rich in good deeds, and to be *generous and ready to share*" (1 Tim 6:18).

3. Enthusiastic, not grudging.

   - "They [the Macedonians] *urgently pleaded with us* for the privilege of sharing in this service for God's people" (2 Cor 8:4).

   - "Now finish the work, so that your *eager willingness* to do it may be matched by your completing it, according to your means" (2 Cor 8:11).

   - "God loves a *cheerful* giver" (2 Cor 9:7; cf. Deut 15:10).

4. Deliberate, not haphazard.

- "The disciples [in Antioch] *decided* that as each one was able, they would send relief to the brothers and sisters living in Judea" (Acts 11:29).

- "Each of you should give what you have *decided in your heart* to give, not reluctantly or under compulsion" (2 Cor 9:7).

5. Regular, not spasmodic.

   - "*On the first day of every week* (= Sunday) each one of you should put aside at home and save whatever extra you earn" (1 Cor 16:2; cf. John 20:1, 19; Acts 20:7).

6. Realistic, not reckless. God does not expect his stewards to give what they do not have or to promise what they are unlikely to afford. Paul's gentile churches did not undertake to bring relief to all the inhabitants in Jerusalem, Jew and Christian alike, but only to "the poor among God's people in Jerusalem" (Rom 15:26).

   - "There was not a needy person among them [in the Jerusalem church], for from time to time as many as owned land or houses sold them, brought the money from the sales, and laid it at the disciples' feet, and *it was distributed to each as any had need*" (Acts 4:34–35).

   - "Which of you, intending to build a tower, does not first *sit down and estimate the cost* to see if you have enough money to complete it?" (Luke 14:28).

   - "The disciples [in Antioch], *as each one was able*, decided to send relief to the brothers and sisters living in Judea" (Acts 11:29).

We see in 1 Cor 16:2, "Each one of you should put aside and save at home" . . .

   - "whatever he can afford" (REB).
   - "whatever extra you earn" (NRSV).

- "a sum of money in keeping with your income" (NIV).

- "in proportion to his gains" (NEB).

- "in proportion to what you have earned" (GNT).

- "as much as each can spare" (NJB).

Literally, the relevant phrase may be rendered "with regard to whatever way he is prospering [*ho ti ean euodōtai*]." The proportion is not some percentage but conformity to whatever degree of prosperity one has enjoyed. A similar sentiment is expressed in two passages in 2 Cor 8: giving is to be "*as resources permit*" (2 Cor 8:11) or "according to/*in proportion to whatever one has*" (2 Cor 8:12). Compare Exod 36:1–7; Deut 16:17.

However, occasional disproportionate giving—that is, giving beyond one's actual resources (2 Cor 8:3)—is a tribute and testimony to God's grace (2 Cor 8:1–2); witness the case of these Macedonians who gave "even beyond their ability" as "their extreme poverty welled up in rich generosity." Yet if such disproportionate giving were the norm, resources for giving would be rapidly depleted (2 Cor 9:10 notwithstanding).

7. Creative, not unimaginative. But care needs to be exercised to ensure that the recipients of any gifts are demonstrably reputable people or causes.

   - "The kingdom of heaven is like a man going on a journey, who summoned his slaves and entrusted his wealth to them. To one he gave five talents, to another two, and to another one, each according to his business ability. Then he went on his journey. The man who had received the five talents *went off at once and traded with them* and made a profit of five more talents. . . . After a long time the master of those slaves returned and settled accounts with them. The one who had received the five talents came forward with the five additional talents. . . . His master said to him, 'Well done, good and trustworthy slave! . . . Come and share your master's happiness!'" (Matt 25:14–16, 19–21).

(A talent was worth more than fifteen years' wages of a laborer).

At the end of the parable of the shrewd manager:

- "The master commended the dishonest manager *because he had acted shrewdly. . . .* I tell you, use worldly wealth to gain friends for yourselves, so that when it is gone, you will be welcomed into eternal dwellings" (Luke 16:8–9).

8. Unobtrusive, not ostentatious.

- "Be careful not to practice your righteousness *in front of others to be seen by them.* If you do, you will have no reward from your Father in heaven" (Matt 6:1).

- "On the first day of every week, each one of you should put aside *at home* [*par' heautō*] whatever extra you earn, saving it up" (1 Cor 16:2; but see Acts 4:35; 5:2; 2 Cor 8:24).

E. IS TITHING A CHRISTIAN OBLIGATION?

To find NT support for the practice of giving one-tenth of our earnings to God, appeal is sometimes made to Heb 7:1–10, which establishes the truth that the payment of tithes to God by mortals acknowledges his total superiority and prompts his blessing: "It is beyond dispute that the inferior person [who pays tithes] is blessed by the superior" (Heb 7:7). But it is equally clear that in these ten verses the focus is not on the secondary matter of tithing but on the superiority of the priesthood of Melchizedek over the Levitical priesthood with a view to establishing the ultimate superiority of Christ's priesthood (Heb 7:20–28). So then, is tithing a spiritual principle of permanent relevance and application (cf. Mal 3:7–10)?

The history of tithing in Israel is complex. When Abram gave Melchizedek "a tenth of everything" (Gen 14:20), this came from the spoils of war (Gen 14:13–16), not from the land's produce of grain or fruit or the first fruits of the herd and flock (Lev 27:30, 32). During OT times, a "triple tithe" developed: (1) a produce tithe (Deut 12:17–18; 14:22–26) to be consumed in the presence of the Lord; (2) a tithe in support of the Levites (Num 18:21–32; Deut 14:27–29); and (3) a goodwill tithe, paid every three years (Deut 14:28–29). Even with variations in these three tithes over time and their possible partial overlap, it is unlikely that the OT tithe amounted to merely 10 percent—it may have been as high as 20 percent or more! In any case, the Jews were obliged to tithe all of their acquired possessions such as crops and livestock (Lev 27:30–33) and not simply their monetary income. All these tithes were not a freewill offering (such as Deut 16:10, 17), but a tax, even a compulsory royal tax (1 Sam 8:10, 15, 17). Departure from covenantal obligations by withholding tithes brought on an ominous divine curse (Mal 3:6–10)—a fact overlooked by those who appeal to this passage to support tithing in the NT era. In late pre-Christian times, a temple tax of two drachmas (= half a shekel) was levied on every male Jew aged between twenty and fifty to support the temple and its services (cf. Matt 17:24–27).

Over the centuries, many believers and churches have been spiritually invigorated when individuals began to honor God by tithing. Also, tithers tend to be better stewards of the nine-tenths than non-tithers are of the ten-tenths. Undoubtedly, we may regard the practice of tithing as a splendid way to begin the adventure of giving to God.

The three NT passages (Matt 23:23 [= Luke 11:42]; Luke 18:12; Heb 7:4–6, 8–9) that explicitly refer to tithing presuppose the OT era and economy, not NT times. Only the portions of OT law explicitly reaffirmed in the NT are part of "the law of Christ" (Gal 6:2), but tithing is nowhere reimposed in the NT.

From an economic point of view, to impose tithing (regarded as the giving of 10 percent of all one's income to worthy causes) as a Christian duty is to perpetuate a "rich/poor" inequality, since (at least in the West) tithing favors the rich and penalizes the poor; for some, to tithe is an unreal goal, while for others it is too meager an offering.

The most potent reason Christians should not regard tithing as a binding obligation is the eloquent silence of the NT on the matter. In the principal passages where tithing might have naturally been reimposed as being appropriate or necessary in the present era—namely chapters 8 and 9 of 2 Cor that deal with giving—we find instead a repeated emphasis on giving voluntarily, generously and proportionately in response to God's limitless giving (see D above). For Paul, giving was not to be dictated by or restricted to a percentage: it was to be "as resources permit" (2 Cor 8:11) or "in proportion to whatever one has" (2 Cor 8:12). Faithfulness in stewardship is better gauged by the wise use of the nine-tenths than even by the regular giving of the one-tenth.

With all this said, it remains significant and undeniable that when believers faithfully and enthusiastically tithe, God's rich blessing naturally follows, his name is honored, and one's spiritual life is invigorated, so that the practice can be confidently proposed as an admirable initial way of honoring God with one's finances.

F. THE RESULTS OF STEWARDSHIP

1. God is pleased, honored, and praised by the generous action of trustworthy stewards. All giving is conducted under God's omniscient gaze. Whatever is the motivation of the giver of a gift and whatever is the reaction of its recipient, God is the final adjudicator of the gift's value. To fail to give to God what he requires is to rob him (Mal 3:8–9). But to give him what he requires or requests from us is to please him and bring him honor and praise.

   - "Cornelius stared at him [an angel of God] in terror. 'What is it, Lord?' he asked. The angel answered, 'Your prayers and gifts to the poor have come up as *a memorial offering before God*'" (Acts 10:4).

   - "This service that you perform is not only supplying the needs of God's people but is also overflowing in *many expressions of thanks to God*" (2 Cor 9:12).

- "I am amply supplied, now that I have received from Epaphroditus the gifts you sent. They are a fragrant offering, *an acceptable sacrifice, pleasing to God*" (Phil 4:18).

- "Do not neglect to do good and to share what you have, for with such sacrifices God is pleased" (Heb 13:16).

- "Whoever serves should do so with the strength God provides, so that in all things *God may be praised* through Jesus Christ" (1 Peter 4:11; cf. Prov 14:31, "Whoever is kind to the needy honors God").

2. By beneficent stewardship the needs of others are met and an example is afforded for others to follow.

- "At the present time your plenty will supply *what they need*, so that in turn their plenty will supply *what you need*" (2 Cor 8:14).

- "I know your eagerness to help, and *I have been boasting about it* to the Macedonians, telling them that since last year you in Achaia were ready to give; and *your enthusiasm has stirred most of them to action*" (2 Cor 9:2).

3. When a steward is trustworthy and gives lavishly, personal needs and resources for further giving are provided by God. It is impossible to out-give God.

- *"Give, and it will be given to you.* A good measure, pressed down, shaken together and running over, will be poured into your lap. *For the measure you give will be the measure you get back*" (Luke 6:38).

- To the generous Philippians (Phil 4:15–16, 18) Paul says, "*My God will fully meet all your needs* in accordance with his glorious bounty in Christ Jesus" (Phil 4:19).

- "Whoever sows generously will also reap generously. . . . And *God is able to bless you abundantly*, so that in all things and at all times, having all that you need, you will abound in every good work" (2 Cor 9:6, 8; cf. Deut 15:10).

4. Faithfulness in the stewardship of one's life, abilities, and possessions prompts the answering of prayer.

- "Dear friends, if our hearts do not condemn us, we have confidence before God and *receive from him anything we ask, because we* keep his commands and *do what pleases him*" (1 John 3:21–22; cf. Prov 21:13; Isa 58:6–9).

5. Faithful stewards are spiritually enriched at present and will be rewarded by God.

- "When you give to the needy, do not let your left hand know what your right hand is doing, so that your giving may be in secret. *Then your Father*, who sees what is done in secret, *will reward you*" (Matt 6:3–4).

- "In everything I did, I showed you that by this kind of hard work we must help the weak, remembering the words the Lord Jesus himself said: '*It is more blessed to give* than to receive" (Acts 20:35; cf. Prov 11:24–25; 28:27.)

- "[Slaves,] serve wholeheartedly, as if you were actually serving the Lord, not people, because you know that *the Lord will reward each one for whatever good they do*, whether they are slave or free" (Eph 6:7–8).

III.

Practical Application

A. SUGGESTIONS FOR INDIVIDUAL BELIEVERS

1. Keeping **records** of one's financial giving is important, not because it gives prior indication of any "treasure in heaven" nor because it may indicate the size of any future tax refund for gifts to registered charities, but because it permits a regular assessment of amounts given and the identity of the recipients so that suitable adjustments can be made as deemed appropriate.

2. A regular (perhaps quarterly) **evaluation** of one's stewardship in its widest sense—strategic use of talents, time, and possessions—is both necessary and rewarding. It serves as a salutary reminder of a coming assessment before God's or Christ's tribunal (Rom 14:10; 2 Cor 5:10) with the reward of divine praise or its forfeiture (see Harris, *Texts (2)*, 172–74).

3. To leave the disbursement of all of your financial gifts to a church or its missions committee is to rob oneself of the special delight of supporting a fellow believer whose friendship

you have cultivated over time and for whom you have regularly prayed. Such a person may serve full-time in a parachurch ministry that offers community care to the needy (such as the Salvation Army) or that seeks to evangelize students in a tertiary educational institute.

4. No one, not even hard-pressed students or single parents who are struggling financially or destitute widows, should regard themselves as unable to contribute in some small way to the flourishing of God's kingdom. (See Luke 21:1–4; 2 Cor 8:1–4.)

5. It has become a pattern for those of us in the West to receive regular requests for financial aid for those facing desperate need as a result of famine, earthquake, or war. Such requests should not override a pattern of giving already carefully planned—that hopefully includes some "disaster relief."

6. No giving can match the pleasure that results from the ongoing financial support of a child or children in the Majority World facilitated by a recognized and reputable agency (such as Tearfund or Barnabas Aid) that works in collaboration with local churches. Regular correspondence between the sponsored child and their sponsor consolidates the relationship.

7. Every believer should always have readily available for use brief, attractive summaries of the gospel that can be given to friends who have expressed an interest in learning about Christianity or who need to learn about its essence. Of the many such small booklets or books, mention may be made of *Becoming a Christian* by John R. W. Stott (InterVarsity Press), *Why Jesus?* by Nicky Gumbel (Alpha International), or my two small books, *John 3:16: What's It All About?* (Wipf & Stock) and *Three Crucial Questions About Jesus* (Wipf & Stock).

8. Use of one's time, energy, and specialist talents is appropriate in such enterprises as ongoing community efforts to provide meals for the needy, to offer advice for those in poverty, and to help rebuild communities that are recovering from natural disasters.

9. An example of creative stewardship: Beneficial outreach is possible if, after developing a friendship with someone who has regularly helped you (such as a checkout worker) or having benefitted from the help of a salesperson (such as a car dealer), you write a formal letter of warm gratitude to that person's manager and send a copy of that letter to the salesperson or checkout assistant themselves, along with a copy of a book or booklet such as one mentioned in # 6 above. On one such occasion the beneficiary of the formal letter told me with great glee that the manager had posted the letter on the staff noticeboard!

10. With regard to establishing priorities for financial provision, two NT passages are relevant.

- "Anyone who does not provide for their relatives, and *especially* for their immediate family, has denied the faith and is worse than an unbeliever" (1 Tim 5:8).
- "As we have opportunity, let us work for the good of all people, *especially* for those who belong to the family of believers" (Gal 6:10).

Priorities:

   i. immediate family and relatives (physical family)

   ii. family of believers (spiritual family)

   iii. all people (human family)

11. On at least one occasion during one's life, it should prove possible for most people to make a substantial gift to a Christian cause of strategic importance. For an example of such a gift, see below, pp. 79–80.

B. SUGGESTIONS FOR CHURCH LEADERS

1. Statistics suggest that 75 percent of a church's income comes from only about 10 percent of church members—usually those with secure and well-paid employment. This estimate underlines the importance of the whole church hearing regular biblical teaching (at least twice a year) about stewardship in general and financial giving in particular. The most appropriate person to provide such teaching is a well-informed elder or deacon so as to avoid any suggestion that the pastor or priest is simply feathering their own nest!

2. Responsibility for the daily administration of a church's finances should ideally be entrusted to a small finance committee with representation from the elders, pastors, and the wider congregation, especially those with specialist training in accounting or business administration. This group could also administer an "emergency fund" that is designed to meet urgent and unexpected needs of church members.

   It may be informative for this committee to calculate the cost per adult church member to provide the facilities that members enjoy, a cost that will inevitably be higher than an imagined "pew rent." Members or regular attendees who feel they cannot contribute financially could contribute other ways, such as dispensing morning teas, doing church cleaning, or driving people to appointments.

3. Detailed reporting to the whole church of its total financial situation is essential, at both the Annual General Meeting and a second biannual meeting, carried out either by the chairperson of the finance committee or its spokesperson. Often a comparison with previous years makes projections for the future illuminating. Equally important are reports about volunteer community projects such as free meals for the needy, providing clothing for the homeless, advice for young families (such as Christians Against Poverty), or hospitality for visitors.

4. In modern times monetary contributions to the church often come via technology. But an essential ingredient of the regular weekly service should be the formal inclusion of a visible offering to God of personal donations of some sort. Even those who contribute remotely could place a coin or some representative token in the offering receptacle to illustrate visibly their surrender to God of all their possessions or of a particular regular gift. What better way for children to dramatize or symbolize their decision to give to God a portion of their weekly or monthly allowance! It is distressing to see an offering bag passed along rows only to be met by the polite shaking of heads. The physical and visual presentation to God of our offerings is an essential part of our worship.

   One way to enable such an offering would be for everyone to be given some representative small token (such as the smallest and least valuable coin) on entering church that could later be placed in the offering bag as a symbol of giving to God. "Now, as we collect these tokens, let us all engage in this physical act of worship as we privately thank our Lord for his many gifts and symbolically bring our financial gifts and surrender our whole lives to him—talents, time, and possessions." Obviously, the same small tokens could be used repeatedly.

5. To promote awareness of the worldwide church, personal and financial links could be established between suburban churches and needy inner-city congregations, and between churches in the affluent West and struggling persecuted Christian assemblies in the Majority World. In Parts One and Two, we have seen Paul's innovative foray into international relief aid. Widely scattered, largely gentile Christian communities within the Roman Empire were creating a relief package for some needy Jewish brothers and sisters whom they had never met.

   When such links had been established, representatives of the "mother church" could regularly visit the adopted "daughter church" to deliver an accumulated gift in person, provide

teaching, stimulate local initiatives in outreach, and then report back to the sending congregation. But any relationship
between churches should be mutual. Mothers benefit from
the insight and gentle provocation of daughters! Now that the
numerical center of gravity in the Christian world has shifted
to Asia, Africa, and Latin America, hopefully this reciprocity
will develop more and more rapidly. In many modern secular
societies, there is a splendid precedent for such a reciprocal
relationship when one town or city is partnered with a similar overseas equivalent, prompting mutual visits and support,
such as regular student exchanges.

6. Specialist seminars could be made regularly available, cover-
ing topics such as personal financial planning, the creation of
wills, or endowment procedures.

7. God's creation mandate (Gen 1:28) could be celebrated by the
planting of trees or shrubs in the church grounds.

8. "Pledge cards," in which church members or regular attendees indicate (in a responsible way) their annual planned giving to the church, can be useful for budget formulation and
can enhance a sense of belonging to a vibrant community.
However, such commitments should not prevent the spon-
taneous joy of giving to meet an unexpected but legitimate
need. Also, sometimes the pledge card may be used to fund a
specific church-sponsored one-off project such as a building
renovation or extension or a missions program.

C. STEWARDSHIP IN ACTION

1. Book Donation

May I be permitted to give a personal illustration of a book donation to a Christian cause of strategic importance?

It is very tempting for a tertiary-level teacher who is about
to retire to make special provision for retirement by selling their

personal library, built up over many years, to a local institution that already has considerable library holdings. But having been closely associated with international students in my nineteen years at Trinity Evangelical Divinity School in Illinois, USA—and being an international myself—I believed it would be strategically important to gift my library to some Majority World theological seminary. Since one of my doctoral students, Dr. David Kasali, was returning to Nairobi, Kenya, as Principal of the Nairobi Evangelical School of Theology (NEGST) (now part of the African National University), it was natural that I should offer the library to his school. So it was that in 1996, just before our return to New Zealand, we contacted the Overseas Council for Theological Education and Missions in the US who generously agreed to pack up and dispatch the 5,600 books and seven hundred journals. Jack Graves, the director of research at the Overseas Council, commented that the gift "will make NEGST the best-equipped New Testament research library on the African continent." The gift helped the institution gain recognition from the Kenyan government for their PhD program in biblical studies. Then in 2015, the Leadership Development/ Langham Partnership in New Zealand fulfilled the same service for a further 1,400 volumes. An insert was pasted inside each of the seven thousand volumes indicating that the books were given in honor of Rev. Zefania Kasali (1915–96), David's father, who had been a pioneering evangelist and pastor in Kenya.

It has given us great pleasure to know that the books were being given a second life in an institution committed to the preparation of leaders for the African church. To cap off the donation, my wife provided two magnificent nine-foot-high quilted banners reading "Look up at the heavens and count the stars" and "Yours, O Lord, is the greatness and the power."

More recently, a further eighty-nine technical books have been donated to the South Asia Institute for Advanced Christian Studies (SAIACS) and a theological college in Myanmar.

2. Lydia and the Church in Philippi

An example of how the faithful stewardship of one person can have a beneficial effect on a whole church may be found in the life of Lydia, a woman of Thyatira in western Asia Minor who was currently living in Philippi. The historian and Gospel writer Luke describes her conversion in Acts 16:13-15. Since ten male heads of households were unavailable in Philippi to form a synagogue, a number of female "worshipers of God" (cf. v. 14) like Lydia had gathered at a nearby river on the Sabbath to engage in Jewish worship which would have included readings from the Law and the Prophets. Undoubtedly, this was an appropriate setting for "Paul's message" about repentance and belief in the Messiah Jesus followed by baptism (v. 15), a message that Lydia and the members of her household embraced.

Being the head of a household (Acts 16:15) as a woman who was either widowed or unmarried and "a trader in [the renowned Lydian] purple cloth" (*porphyropōlis*, Acts 16:14), Lydia was not only a woman of rank (cf. Acts 17:4, 12) but also a woman of wealth; also witness the fact that she invited Paul, Silas, and Luke to stay in her home (Acts 16:15) which was large enough to serve as the Philippian house church (Acts 16:40). The church grew from its infancy in about AD 49 (described in Acts 16) to its maturity in about AD 61 when Paul wrote his letter (Philippians) to the church from his prison in Rome. By that time there were "overseers and deacons" in the Philippian church (Phil 1:1). There is no mention of Lydia in Philippians (unless the unnamed "my true companion" in Phil 4:3 refers to her); she may have died or moved elsewhere in connection with her trade.

It is a fair inference—although still an inference—that Lydia's role as a faithful steward who was given to hospitality and (thus presumably) financial generosity partly accounts for the unique reputation of the Philippians as financial supporters of Paul in his ministry:

> As you Philippians know, in the early days of your
> acquaintance with the gospel, when I set out from

Macedonia, not one church shared with me in the matter of giving and receiving, except you only, for even when I was in Thessalonica, you sent me help more than once when I was in need. . . . I have been paid in full and have more than enough. I am fully supplied, now that I have received from Epaphroditus the gifts you sent. They are a fragrant offering, a sacrifice acceptable and pleasing to God. (Phil 4:15–16, 18)

D. CONCLUSION

"We are permanently in debt but never bankrupt."

Contained in that striking maxim are several basic truths about stewardship. Humans are permanently indebted to the supreme Master, the one who created them, sustains their lives, and gave them a gift so generous that it can never be exhaustively described—the Messiah, Jesus Christ (2 Cor 9:15). But while those debts cannot ever be fully repaid, we always have at our disposal some resources to repay our debts in part and so avoid bankruptcy. Those resources that are to be used for the benefit of others and the praise of God include God-given personal giftings, restricted time, and limited assets. We are grateful debtors who will never have to declare insolvency. As responsible stewards, we seek to multiply our Master's investments and so provide him with handsome dividends.

Bibliography

Anderson, Gary A. *Charity: The Place of the Poor in the Biblical Tradition.* New Haven: Yale University Press, 2013.

Beckheuer, Burkhard. *Paulus und Jerusalem: Kollekte und Mission im theologischen Denken des Heidenapostels.* Frankfurt: Lang, 1997.

Betz, Hans D. *2 Corinthians 8–9: A Commentary on Two Administrative Letters of the Apostle Paul.* Philadelphia: Fortress, 1985.

Downs, David J. *The Offering of the Gentiles: Paul's Collection for Jerusalem in Its Chronological, Cultural, and Cultic Contexts.* Grand Rapids: Eerdmans, 2016.

Georgi, Dieter. *Remembering the Poor: The History of Paul's Collection for Jerusalem.* Nashville: Abingdon, 1992.

Graham, Daryn. "The Genesis of the Jerusalem Donation." *Themelios* 45.1 (2023).

Harris, Murray J. *Renowned—But . . . : The Church of Corinth in the First Century AD and Its Relevance for the Twenty-First-Century Church.* Eugene, OR: Wipf and Stock, 2022.

Hock, R. F. *The Social Context of Paul's Ministry: Tentmaking and Apostleship.* Minneapolis: Fortress, 2007.

Johnson, Luke T. *Sharing Possessions: What Faith Demands.* Grand Rapids: Eerdmans, 2011.

Joubert, Stephan. *Paul as Benefactor: Reciprocity, Strategy and Theological Reflection in Paul's Collection.* Tübingen: Mohr Siebeck, 2000.

Kim, Byung-Mo. *Die paulinische Kollekte.* Tübingen: Francke, 2002.

Longenecker, Bruce W. *Remember the Poor: Paul, Poverty, and the Greco-Roman World.* Grand Rapids: Eerdmans, 2010.

Meeks, W. A. *The First Urban Christians: The Social World of the Apostle Paul.* New Haven: Yale University Press, 1983.

Meggitt, Justin. *Paul, Poverty and Survival: Studies of the New Testament and Its World.* Edinburgh: T & T Clark, 1998.

Murray, Stuart. *Beyond Tithing.* Carlisle: Paternoster, 2002.

Nickle, Keith. *The Collection: A Study in Paul's Strategy.* Naperville, IL: Allenson, 1966.

O'Mahoney, Kieran J. *Pauline Persuasion: A Sounding in 2 Corinthians 8–9.* Sheffield: Sheffield Academic, 2000.

Verbrugge, Verlyn D. *Paul's Style of Church Leadership Illustrated by His Instructions to the Corinthians on the Collection.* San Francisco: Mellen Research University Press, 1992.

Welborn, L. L. "'That There May Be Equality': The Contexts and Consequences of a Pauline Ideal." *New Testament Studies* 59 (2013) 73–90.

Wheeler, Sandra E. *Wealth as Peril and Obligation: The New Testament on Possessions.* Grand Rapids: Eerdmans, 1995.

www.ingramcontent.com/pod-product-compliance
Lightning Source LLC
Chambersburg PA
CBHW060419090426
42734CB00011B/2376